AF705415

IB BUSINESS MANAGEMENT

Internal Assessment

IB BUSINESS MANAGEMENT

Internal Assessment

The Definitive Business Management [HL/SL] IA
Guide For the International Baccalaureate [IB] Diploma

Seba Ismail

Zouev IB Publishing

This book is printed on acid-free paper.

Published 2023

Printed by Zouev IB Publishing

ISBN 978-1-9996115-8-3, paperback.

TABLE OF CONTENTS

PART I

THE BUSINESS MANAGEMENT IA GUIDE

1. INTRODUCTION

The Business Management (BM) IA is one of the most dynamic, easily applied, and interesting IA amongst the subjects that the IB offers its students. In addition to that, the IA is a vital component of your final grade in the IB, it is a huge opportunity to take accountability of your learning and show off the knowledge you have gained from the course to your teachers (and examiners)!

The first step to commence the process of working towards progressing through your IA is to distinguish the level at which you take the course, whether it is at a standard level (SL), or a higher level (HL).[1] Which, there are minor differences between the requirements for each. Regarding SL students, they will need to depend on secondary research to develop a written commentary on a well-known company; preferably a public-limited company.

HL students, need to depend on primary research to complete a research project on a business they have primary access to, such as your uncle's car business, your cousin's jewelry store, or your mother's flower shop. However, some students do not have access to such an opportunity. For that, I would recommend finding a business you can easily contact and ensure that you can get adequate data from.

But... what should I do now?

Well, after you've chosen a business, you should be able to identify and explore an issue that the business is facing. You will be able to deduce this information from your research; if you are an SL student, or from a quick interview with the CEO, managers, or employees, if you are an HL student.

---

[1] *It is important to note that both SL and HL IA weightings are 25% of the final grade for May 2023 students.

Apart from the promising knowledge and understanding that you will gain from the IA, you will also have the opportunity to develop your scope in various ATL skills, such as critical thinking skills to effectively identify an issue as well as propose possible and realistic solutions for businesses to follow to help minimize the consequences that might have resulted from the challenges they are facing. As well as communication in terms of the written language in your IA to exchange information with the reader in an effective manner. Not only that, but certain aspects of research will surely develop in the process or way of obtaining information.

This is a general introduction to the BM IA, continuing this guide will aim to help you structure, your IA according to your level, explain the criteria briefly, provide an insight into the mandatory sections to include in your IA, and tips and tricks that will help you score top marks from an IB alumni!

2. HOW TO STRUCTURE YOUR BUSINESS MANAGEMENT IA?

The following content presents a recommended structure to follow in completing your BM IA. This will ensure that you are meeting the needs of the criteria only if you follow through thoroughly. Note that for SL and HL students the structure differs, so only follow what applies to you! The table below briefly states the few differences between each structure:

SL	**HL**
Word count is 1500 and the research proposal is not graded but can be used for guidance to influence your research in the right way.	Word count is individually customized to each component. The research proposal should be 500 words, and the written report should not exceed 2000 words (including the executive summary that should not exceed 200 words).
Most/all the data should be obtained from a few supporting documents; 3-5 is ideal	HL students can use unlimited sources, as there isn't an ideal number of sources to use.

and it should not be more than that, so choose wisely.	
Relies heavily on secondary research.	Relies heavily on primary research.

Listed below is lay out of the recommended structure for SL students firstly:

Title page:

Business Management (name of the subject)

Standard level (the level at which you study the course)

Internal assessment

Examination session (May 2023)

Research question

Anticipated audience (example: to Company ABC LTD)

IA word count

Contents page:

Acknowledgements:

This section is not included in the word count, and it is not mandatory to include it, but generally it can be a nice gesture to thank those who have helped you complete your research.

Introduction:

(About 150 words), here you should be able to explain the function of the company, as well as provide an explanation for your research question and the importance of it for the company.

Methodology:

(About 200 words), you should include the parts/tools that you will use from the content to complete your research and explain the sources (supporting documents) you will use that will help work towards answering your research question. Moreover, you should explain the methods you think are ideal to collect data and analyze it. As well as identify possible difficulties and offer realistic solutions that will minimize consequences on your research.

You can organize these sections in a table format as follows (this is applied for HL students as well, in the methodology employed section that is discussed later):

Syllabus unit	**Areas to be covered**	**Reason**
1.3 Organizational Objectives	SWOT Matrix	Identify strengths, weaknesses, opportunities, and threats that are relatable to the business. [2]

Type of source	**Source**	**Reason**
Secondary	Statistics regarding those who enjoy drinking Pepsi's products.	To examine whether Pepsi should go on with the decision to make their signature baked goods instead of expanding the flavors of their fizzy drinks. [3]

Technique	**Reason**

[2] Parts/ tools from the content that will be used for research.
[3] Sources that will be used for research and how it will be employed **(HL students should use this in their methodology employed section).**

1.3 Organizational Objectives: SWOT Matrix	Examine the status of the business internally and externally. [4]

Anticipated Difficulties	Possible solutions
Financial statements can be different in many web pages due to the company being public limited.	Find web sites that are only authorized by the company to publish their financial accounts. [5]

Analysis and Discussion:

(About 900 words), I would like to call this part of the investigation the "meat!" This is where you analyze and discuss the findings and results of the research you conducted. I am sure you've come across various writing techniques to make this part effective and successful, such as PEEL. However, a personal favorite is JAM (especially on toast)! Jokes aside, it is an effective tool to plan your writing in terms of justification and analysis. It stands for Justification, Analysis, and Mini conclusion.

Let's break down the contents of the JAM method. [6]

Primarily, you need to focus on the "J," for example, if you're doing a SWOT analysis for your company, ask yourself why do you need the SWOT "specifically" to answer your research question. You can start phrasing it like, the depth of the SWOT analysis is suitable for the research question because … (fill in the blanks)! For "A," you should consider filling in the SWOT matrix, what does the company have that make it strong? Are there any threats that the company might face in the near future, like the rise of the rivals or competition? Finally, you should consider deducing a mini conclusion, of what you can identify from the SWOT matrix that you've conducted, should the company relocate to avoid clashes with the

---

[4] This is a way to lay out the methods for data collection and analysis used in your research and how it will be employed **(HL students should use this in their methodology employed section).**

[5] Difficulties and solutions that one will face in their research.

[6] The JAM method is also applicable for HL students in the Analysis and Discussion section.

neighborhood? Should they proceed with the merge that company "Y" is offering? What potential benefits would that offer? Etc.

Conclusion:

(About 250 words), in this section you should be aware that you are finalizing or highlighting certain points you discussed before, not stating anything new! Think of it as repeating what you've just said but in a different manner, of course. This is the section where the reader is waiting for a well-defined response to your research question. You can also touch on the pros and cons of the tools you came up with to help in the completion of the research and the limitations that you might have had to pay close attention to.

Works cited:

(Not included in the word count), this is where you should cite the authors and web pages of where you retrieved your information from (your 3-5 supporting documents). This should be clearly cited in whatever style your school recommends for you to do, whether its APA, MLA, IEEE, etc.

Appendices:

This is a section in the IA where you need to provide snapshots of the sources, images or any tool that helped gather information to aid in your research. Throughout the IA, you can refer to your appendices as "appendix 1," or "see supporting document 3" for instance.

The following is a lay out of the recommended structure for HL students:

Title page:

Business Management (name of the subject)

Higher level (the level at which you study the course)

Internal assessment

Examination session (May 2023)

Research question

Research proposal word count: (…/500 words)

Executive summary word count: (…/200 words)

Written report word count: (…/2000 words)

Research proposal:

Research question.

Rationale for study: here you should be able to briefly discuss who the company is? What is the issue/ area you're willing to provide a solution for?

Methodology:

The contents of this section is similar to the SL students' in many ways. Such as, mentioning the areas of the syllabus to be covered, possible sources of information, methods for data collection and analysis, and anticipated difficulties and proposed possible solutions, these can be listed as the table method to make it easier to follow along and to organize, as it was mentioned above. In addition to that, the methodology for HL students should contain the following information, organizations and individuals to be approached, and an action plan explaining briefly the task with deadlines:

Name	Position in "ZYX business"
John David	CEO of ZYX business [7]

Task	Deadline
Construct a survey for the employees of ZYX business	20/12/2022[8]

Written report – contents of research project:

[7] Organizations and individuals to be approached table format.

[8] Action plan exemplar format.

You can write this section of the report according to the following format:

This research project aims to help **(*insert name of the company*)** decide if implementing **(*insert name of the strategy proposed*)** to solve their **(*insert the main issue you are facing/your research is focusing on*).**

It answers the following research question:

(*insert RQ here*).

The intended audience is:

(*insert the name of the founders/employees/managers of the company and HL IA supervisor*).

Acknowledgements:

This section is not included in the word count, here you thank those who have helped you complete your research such as your HL IA supervisor and employees/managers that gave you their time to complete your project.

Table of contents page:

After the acknowledgements section be sure to add a table of contents page with page numbers and include the following contents of the written report such as an executive summary, introduction, the methodology employed, main results and findings, analysis and discussion, conclusion, recommendation, works cited, and appendices.

Executive summary:

(About 200 words). You will need to give a quick and brief account of the type of business you are basing your investigation on and the main issue they are facing, as well as the root cause of it. Then you should be able to evaluate the decision you are proposing to the company, to solve the main issue, they are facing. Afterwards, you should state how you came up with the decision; this might have been developed from an interview with the founder, a questionnaire for the customers, or employees' responses to a survey. Finally, you should be able to give a brief recommendation for why they should implement the suggestion you are proposing to the business.

Introduction:

(About 200 words). You might have felt that this section repeats itself from the rationale of the study, however, in the introduction you should focus on giving a detailed account of the business and its functions. You can discuss things such as how many founders are there, how many years they've been in the business, are they based in the city or the countryside. Are they in tune with their customers? What are their products mostly about? You should also mention their recent goals or objectives and issues. Finally, you should mention your research question again.

Methodology employed:

This can be organized in a table format that was displayed earlier on the previous pages. This is where you state the "technique," which is the tool from the content you used to explain the application and relevance of it to the business in your research. Additionally, you will need to design another table outlining the type of source you used; being primary. As well as, the source of where you obtained the information, and finally explaining a reason for the importance of it.

Main Results and Findings:

In this section, you are required to discuss and process the data or information that you collected from your research, such as interviews you've conducted with the founders, questionnaires you sent out to the employees and/or customers to find out their satisfaction, or highlights from a secondary resource to help you collect relevant information and that will aid in your research. Please be aware that this is not yet the part where you discuss and apply the tools you used from the content just yet, this segment is a bit earlier! Also, you might have realized that the requirements of this segment of the research project are different to that of the SL's.

Analysis and Discussion:

Now, this is where the fun commences! Here you will get the chance to apply the knowledge you've learnt and the tools you've used in class to your chosen business. You will follow three basic steps, to identify, analyze, discuss and/or explain. Or, to make your lives much easier you can use the JAM method that was discussed above in the SL section. Let's say you're doing a PEST analysis for the company "CDE," and their focus is on health and wellness, you'll need to firstly identify the political, economic, social, and technological factors affecting the business in the present time or the near future. Next, you should fill in the table which is where the analysis part comes in. So, is the country in which CDE is operating politically stable or unstable? Are taxes at an attainable rate? Is there a growing demand for the healthy products CDE is selling? Does the company have a social media account? Is there reliable internet access where the company is established so that it is user-friendly? Finally, you should consider the discussion or explanation process. In which you would dig in to find the why for the points you've analyzed. For example, country X in which CDE is established is politically stable, this, in turn, would serve CDE a great advantage as it will attract external stakeholders such as investors, and customers; especially to be a source of their satisfaction and trust. A very important point to consider is to organize this section where the qualitative tools come first and quantitative comes second, please note that you need at least one financial tool.

Conclusion:

The conclusion aims to finalize or highlight the main points that were discussed throughout the investigation. Ask yourself some questions about the highlights of your findings, for example, what do the findings with the CEO of company "H" illustrate? How are they marketing their products? Is it effective? Are their social media accounts well-monitored and are they constantly up to date? Are their marketing strategies ethical? These are only example questions to help you think about writing down your own final words. But you're only touching up again on the important points not noting something new. So, keep that in mind!

Recommendation:

This is one of the last steps towards finalizing your investigation. Based on the findings you've deduced, should the company persist with the current marketing strategies, or should they implement the new ones? If they should go ahead to implement the new marketing strategies, how can they do it? What are the processes they should follow? What are the possible advantages of the new marketing strategies on the potential and/or targeted customers? Remember, it's just your recommendation based on your knowledge in addition to the application of it to your findings on how the company can solve their issues.

Works cited:

This is where you should cite the authors and web pages of where you retrieved your information from. This should be clearly cited in whatever style your school recommends for you to do, whether its APA, MLA, IEEE, etc. Remember that there are dangers of not completing this section, as you can be accused of plagiarism!

Appendices:

This is a section in the IA where you need to provide snapshots of the sources, images or any tool that helped gather information to aid in your research. Throughout the IA, you can refer to your appendices as "appendix 1," or "see appendix 3."

3. WHAT IS THE PURPOSE FOR THE BM IA SECTIONS?

If you're still here reading this, I am glad. I know the past section was not made as fun as possible, but the main reason was to take you through a step-by-step account of how to excel at each section in your BM IA. Now, you might have a few questions about why you need to include certain sections in your IA, and I can tell you that I was in your shoes a few months ago. Well here, you are definitely in the right place, where your wonders will be fulfilled (hopefully)!

Research question:

Firstly, you start with a research question. And I know that you already know what the importance of a research question is, so as cliché as it may sound, a research question is there to guide you and offer you a focus in your research project/commentary.

I can guarantee that the first written feedback you received on your IA was "Mark, this seems like a good start, but can you make your research question more specific?" Or "Ava, reconsider your research question it's too broad!" I can tell you that you're not the only one! As easy as it may seem to come up with a research question, many things can go wrong in formulating one. Here is a tip to make your research question the best (guaranteed)! Make it specific by looking at one specific issue in the business functions whether it's operations, marketing, HR, finance, etc. Don't try formulating your question around how McDonald's is using gorilla marketing in addition to current organizational structure issues. One, there is no connection between the two, and two, due to choosing your focus to be on different aspects at the same time, you will not be able to make efficient and specific conclusions or analysis due to the broad scope that you chose to have. So, in turn you made your life difficult my friend!

Rationale for study (HL):

This section provides your audience with a clear understanding of the type of business you are investigating, as well as the main issue they're facing. It guides your audience and yourself to help you stay on track with the main points you are covering, tools to help you analyze the situation, and to easily identify a solution for the problem the business is facing.

Introduction:

Although it seems like a simple task to fulfil, it's one to look for. As many students don't know exactly what to say or not in the introduction. This section provides more insight into the nature of the business in which the company operates, as the process in which the idea was initiated and the important figures that helped the business come to life. You are also expected to talk about their main goal/objective for the business. This can be a chance to discuss or state their mission and vision statements. A few other things you can touch on, are their presence. Are they there only in hot seasons, for example on the beaches during the summer? Or, during winter evenings at Christmas when the public is sipping on hot chocolate? It can be all year long too. It is a great opportunity as well to mention the number of years the business has been operating for. Another thing you will state briefly is their recent aims and the issue they are facing. Think of this as re-stating your research question in a clear and concise statement.

Action plan (HL):

The action plan is there to help you visualize the tasks you need to get done and keep you on top of the game. This prevents any slacking that might lead to inefficiently responding to deadlines. It also shows the audience that you've got a firm grip on all the tasks needed to complete the IA.

Methodology/Methodology employed:

This section provides you with a guide on how to apply the tools and the content you've learnt to your own business, take on effective analysis, and draw conclusions or recommendations to show your understanding of your research and apply your knowledge in the real world. This will also act as an organizational tool for your primary/secondary research, as it will allow you to specifically identify what is it that you're looking for in that graphic organizer or the interview with that one customer that was filing complaints against the products sold in the business.

Anticipated Difficulties and Possible Solutions:

Before you start it's always great to plan for the unpleasant surprises before the good ones, and so, this section is serving this need. It doesn't only allow you to come up with a plan B, it grants you a plan H as well! It gives you a basic idea of how you can tackle any situation. For example, if you are asking for a company's financial statement, they can refuse to provide it to you, hence its confidentiality. You can either insist (nicely), by assuring them it's solely for academic purposes and that you are trying to help them in any way (if they have a financial issue). Or you can estimate roughly the main figures so you can come up with your financial reports. This will be an effective solution as it will also show the reader that you are indeed practicing critical thinking.

Acknowledgements:

I will repeat this again and again, this section "is not compulsory" *insert that in capitalized letters.* Yet, it's always a nice gesture to include those who have helped you in your project. It's just a way to explain your gratitude for their guidance and input in your work.

Executive summary (HL):

The executive summary is there to quickly summarize four key points, outlining the problem the business is facing, the tools and knowledge from the content that you applied, touch up on how the information from your research was collected; primary, or secondary, and finally, conclude your findings and based on them recommend/suggest what the business should follow to improve its current situation.

Main results and findings:

This section is for summarizing both primary and secondary research findings. For primary research, any interviews you've conducted, questionnaires or surveys that you've sent out need to be highlighted in this section. This is equally important for secondary research as well, as any statistics you've retrieved online or information about the company's position in comparison to its rivals should all be summarized in this part. This will all be helpful one you are concluding your findings to list down recommendations.

Analysis:

This is a big part of your IA, the main purpose of this section is not to "torture" your brain at all! It is there to help you break down and interpret closely the reason/cause for the information you've collected. It helps you critically think and process your data efficiently so that the solution becomes clearer.

Conclusion:

Here, this section helps you wrap up and highlight the main findings that can get you a clear vision of the recommendation/suggestion that you will provide or propose for the company.

Recommendation:

The recommendation is there to remind you that you are providing a suggestion or "answering" your research question. Here you will answer your research question and evaluate the decision from all aspects.

4. ASSESSMENT CRITERIA

The IA criteria can be a little hard to apply, for that, this section will simplify the requirements and highlight the most prominent understandings to ensure that you will maximize the highest score in each criterion.

By now, you already know that the requirements for HL and SL are different and so are their grading criteria. Below is an explanation of the assessment criteria for both SL and HL.

SL grading criteria are composed of seven assessment criteria, all the way from A to G. It is important to note that the written commentary is out of 25 marks, however, the grades in each criterion are not distributed equally.

Firstly, Criterion A: supporting documents, is assessed out of 4 marks. It merely focuses on whether you have enough and sufficient documents to answer your research question in appropriate detail, from which you can successfully conclude. An important consideration to bear in mind is that the documents should be published for a maximum of three years, before the date of submission. Additionally, it should be carried out in the language of submission, in other words, a Spanish document should not take place in an English-written IA.

Criterion A: Supporting documents

Achievement level	**Level descriptor**
0	The work does not reach standards outlined by the descriptors.
1	There are only one or two, or more than five, supporting documents, or they are of marginal relevance.
2	The supporting documents are generally relevant but some lack depth, or they were published more than three years prior to the submission of the IA to the IB, or they are not all translated in the language of submission.
3	The supporting documents are relevant and sufficiently in-depth.
4	The supporting documents are relevant, sufficiently in-depth and provide a range of ideas and views. [9]

Secondly, Criterion B: Choice and application of tools, techniques, and theories, is assessed out of five marks. It mainly focuses on the degree to which the student properly outlines and explains the relation of the business tools or the content of the Business and Management course, as well as the application of it in the IA. To maximize your grade in this criterion, you need a solid understanding of all the theories and schemes learnt in class.

[9] Note that all the assessment criteria were taken directly from the IB.

Criterion B: choice and application of tools, techniques, and theories

Achievement level	Level descriptor
0	The work does not reach a standard described by the descriptors.
1	There is a limited selection of business management tools, techniques, and theories, and these are not applied.
2	There is a limited selection of business management tools, techniques, and theories, and these are superficially applied.
3	There is an appropriate selection of business management tools, techniques, and theories, but these are superficially applied.
4	There is an appropriate selection of business management tools, techniques and theories, and these are suitably applied.
5	There is an appropriate selection of business management tools, techniques and theories, and these are skillfully applied.

Third, criterion C: Choice and analysis of data and integration of ideas. The maximum achieving grade is a 5 in this criterion. It is mostly associated with the application of the business tools, concepts, and theories that you've identified and their relation to your case.

You are required to think beyond the box, don't just tell the reader the obvious, but state what is beyond that.

Criterion C: Choice and analysis of data and integration of ideas

Achievement level	**Level descriptor**
0	The work does not reach a standard described by the descriptors.
1	There is a limited selection of data from the supporting documents but no analysis.
2	There is a limited selection of data from the supporting documents with superficial analysis.
3	There is an appropriate selection of data from the supporting documents with satisfactory analysis.
4	There is an appropriate selection of data from the supporting documents with good analysis and some integration of ideas.
5	There is an appropriate selection of data from the supporting documents with skillful analysis and a coherent integration of ideas.

Fourth, criterion D: Conclusions. It is marked out of three marks, it mostly focuses on your ability to draw conclusions that are effective, useful, and most importantly relevant. This section should be synchronized with what you have said throughout the essay. Please do not develop new ideas, the conclusions should include what has already existed.

Criterion D: Conclusions

Achievement level	**Level descriptor**
0	The work does not reach a standard described by the descriptors.
1	Conclusions are inconsistent with the evidence presented, or conclusions are superficial.
2	Some conclusions are consistent with the evidence presented.
3	Conclusions are consistent with the evidence presented and explicitly answer the commentary question.

Fifth, criterion E: evaluation, the maximum score in this criterion is a 4. It is concerned with assessing the arguments, findings, and suggestions you have mentioned and discussed throughout the IA.

Criterion E: Evaluation

Achievement level	**Level descriptor**
0	The work does not reach a standard described by the descriptors.
1	There is limited evidence of evaluation
2	There is evidence of evaluation, and some judgments are substantiated.

3	There is evidence of evaluation, and judgments are substantiated.
4	There is thorough evidence of evaluation, and judgments are well substantiated.

Sixth, criterion F: structure, is assessed out of two marks, and it emphasizes a coherent and appropriate organization, that includes all the requirements, as well as, can be followed. Or in other words, follow the structure that was discussed above in this book!

Criterion F: Structure

Achievement level	**Level descriptor**
0	The work does not reach a standard described by the descriptors.
1	Limited structure.
2	Appropriate structure.

Seventh, criterion G: presentation, also has a maximum grade of two. From the name, it explicitly requires students to present the information in an organized manner, involving the correct orientation, such as a table of contents, headings, appropriate titles, page numbers, in-text citations as well as a bibliography, from valuable references (not Wikipedia please)! Make sure you've included all the necessary components in your written commentary. And yes, you will get marked down if you've missed any.

Criterion G: Presentation

Achievement level	**Level descriptor**

0	The work does not reach a standard described by the descriptors.
1	One or more of the above elements of a well presented commentary is missing.
2	All of the above elements of a well presented commentary are included.

It's now time to shift our focus towards the HL requirements. The HL assessment criteria are nine, from A to I. Now, let's take a closer look at the requirements.

Firstly, criterion A: research proposal. It is assessed out of three marks. This criterion solely focuses on the research proposal consisting of the research question and methodology. As it expects the student to carry on an effective procedure with regard to how conclusions will be generated.

Criterion A: Research proposal.

Achievement level	**Level descriptor**
0	The work does not reach a standard described by the descriptors.
1	The research proposal is presented but is generally inappropriate, or two or more elements are missing.
2	The research proposal is generally appropriate but some elements lack clarity, detail and focus, or one element is missing.

3	The research proposal with all the required elements is appropriate, detailed, clear and focused.

Secondly, criterion B: sources and data. It is also assessed out of three marks. It measures the degree to which the student chooses and uses their primary sources efficiently to support the suggestion or the recommendation you are trying to promote.

Criterion B: Sources and data

Achievement level	**Level descriptor**
0	The work does not reach a standard described by the descriptors.
1	Some of the primary sources selected or the data collected are appropriate.
2	The primary sources selected and the data collected are appropriate, but are not varied and sufficient.
3	The primary sources selected and the data collected are appropriate, varied and sufficient.

Third, criterion C: use of tools, techniques, and theories. It has a maximum score of three. The objective of the criterion focuses on the degree to which you understand the situation of your chosen business, as well as, the application of the relevant business tool to your selected business.

Criterion C: Use of tools, techniques, and theories

Achievement level	**Level descriptor**

0	The work does not reach a standard described by the descriptors.
1	There is a limited understanding of business management tools, techniques and theories, and these are not applied or are superficially applied.
2	There is a satisfactory understanding of relevant business management tools, techniques and theories, and these are suitably applied.
3	There is a good understanding of relevant business management tools, techniques and theories, and these are skillfully applied.

Fourth, criterion D: analysis and evaluation. This carries a huge weight in terms of the maximum grade you can score. It is out of six. In short, you should focus on four main aspects. Using relevant business tools and sources of information, justify the chosen tools by relating them to your focus/research question, apply the tools in a coherent matter to your business, and lastly and most importantly, make sure as you're analyzing to evaluate your arguments, as you will be unable to score above a 3 if you haven't made any judgements.

Criterion D: Analysis and evaluation

Achievement level	**Level descriptor**
0	The work does not reach a standard described by the descriptors.
1	The results and findings are limited, and no analysis of them is provided.

2	The results and findings are limited, and a superficial analysis of them is provided.
3	There is a satisfactory analysis of the results and findings and some integration of ideas.
4	There is a satisfactory analysis of the results and findings, a satisfactory integration of ideas and some evidence of evaluation.
5	There is a good analysis of the results and findings, a good integration of ideas and evidence of substantiated evaluation.
6	There is a skillful analysis of the results and findings, a coherent integration of ideas and consistent evidence of substantiated evaluation.

Fifth, criterion E: Conclusion (written report), having a maximum scoring grade of two. As the name suggests, this criterion tests to which degree can one make valid and relevant conclusions. A few things to take into account is to conclude what was already mentioned, conclusions are a place to wrap up what you've previously mentioned but not a place to come up with new ideas. It is also taking more of an evaluative approach, in which you should mention schemes to study further, in other words, what could you have done better.

Criterion E: Conclusion (written report)

Achievement level	**Level descriptor**

0	The work does not reach a standard described by the descriptors.
1	There are some conclusions, but they are unsubstantiated and/or inconsistent with the evidence presented in the main body of the report.
2	Conclusions are substantiated and consistent with the evidence presented in the main body of the report. Areas for further study have been identified, if appropriate.

Sixth, criterion F: recommendations (written report), is also worth a total of two marks. This has to be backed up by evidence, if you are recommending a particular suggestion, you should give a brief explanation of why it is necessary for the context of your business. The recommendation should also be synchronized with your research question. If your research question is focused on improving marketing strategies, a recommendation should cover a specific marketing strategy for example above-the-line or below-the-line.

Criterion F: Recommendation (written report)

Achievement level	**Level descriptor**
0	The work does not reach a standard described by the descriptors.
1	There are recommendations, but they are unsubstantiated and/or inconsistent with the conclusions, or they do not answer the research question.

2	The recommendations are substantiated and consistent with the conclusions, and they answer the research question.

Seventh, criterion G: structure (written report), is worth two marks. The IA should be organized in an easy-to-follow and coherent manner. My recommendation is to simply follow the format that was discussed earlier (this is your way to success)! ☺

Criterion G: Structure (written report)

Achievement level	**Level descriptor**
0	The work does not reach a standard described by the descriptors.
1	Limited structure.
2	Appropriate structure.

Eighth, criterion H: presentation (written report), is also worth two points. I would recommend having a checklist for all the necessary components that should be included in the IA.

Criterion H: Presentation (written report)

Achievement level	**Level descriptor**
0	The work does not reach a standard described by the descriptors.
1	The report is missing one or more of the required components, or the

	components are not in the correct order or format.
2	The report includes all of the required components in the correct order and format.

Ninth, criterion I: reflective thinking (written report), has a maximum grade of two marks as well. This criterion evaluates the degree to which the student can analyze, explain, and evaluate the arguments that they've provided.

Criterion I: Reflective thinking (written report)

Achievement level	**Level descriptor**
0	The work does not reach a standard described by the descriptors.
1	The report includes limited or superficial reflective thinking on the approach taken in this piece of research and its limitations.
2	The report includes appropriate evidence of reflective thinking on the approach taken in this piece of research and its limitations.

5. TIPS AND TRICKS

In this section, I will be sharing the top tips that helped me excel in the Business Management IA. Now, it might all be repetitive, however, it is necessary to remind yourselves of them now and then, especially in a huge project like the IA.

Firstly, and most important, to create a to-do list or a Gantt chart. Especially if you are a visual learner like me, you will find a visual checklist more appealing and useful as it will help you visualize how far you've come in your project and how much more is left, this would be extra helpful if you include dates of completion or at which you would like to achieve the task. As it helps with time management and means of organization.

Secondly, I would recommend finding a topic that does add to your curiosity and interest. Remember, you are stuck with this topic for about a year, so if the topic does not interest you, the IA would cause you the greatest headache.

Third, always always always refer to the criteria and the IA handouts. They are there to guide you and help keep you on track, and that you develop a solid understanding of the requirements to be met. You should also take this book as an opportunity as it explains the IA in a nutshell, which is a chance to tackle.

Next, look at previous IA exemplars, there are excellent examples in this book that can inspire and guide you in the right direction. However, I believe that this advice is a double-edged sword, you can surely feel motivated, but bear in mind that you will need to follow the academic honesty policy and stay away from any malpractices, such as plagiarism.

Make sure to submit your drafts on time. It is a new experience when writing your IA, it's normal to feel confused, puzzled, and frustrated. For that, your teachers have created deadlines so that they can track your progress and give out useful feedback, to guide you in the correct pathway. Even if you have a fraction of what has been assigned, do submit it, and don't be shy to ask for help if you are experiencing any sort of confusion.

Additionally, never forget to cite. At this point, you should be doing it spontaneously, remember these are ways to avoid academic malpractice and it's also a manner in which you are giving credit to where the information was retrieved from.

Moreover, for HL students, when you're conducting interviews or questionnaires, make sure as you're progressing along the way to conclude or highlight shocking, interesting, or new ideas that you might come across. This is an easy way in which you can conclude significant ideas and make a recommendation based on that.

In regards to SL students, when making sure to choose sufficient and significant supporting documents, do put your focus question in front of you and try to jot down a few points here and there. The stronger your points are and the happier you are with them, consider this source for the completion of your IA.

Finally, I hope that the tips and guide were helpful. Remember that the IA should be an enjoyable process, also remember to never doubt yourselves or your capabilities, it might seem impossible now, but remember the reward of it at the end. Good luck!

5. BIBLIOGRAPHY

Alimin, E. (2020, July 26). *Overview: Business Management HL IA* . IBlieve web site : https://iblieve.org/overview-business-management-hl-ia/

IB Biz . (2022). *Tips for a 10 mark response on Paper 2* . IB Biz web site : https://www.ibbiz.org/essay-tips

IB Mastery . (2022). *How to Structure an SL Business Management Internal Assessment* . IB Mastery web site : https://www.ibmastery.com/blog/how-to-structure-an-sl-business-management-internal-assessment

Wilkes, A. (2022, February 7). *Internal Assessment - Business Management* . Library. scotch web site : https://library.scotch.wa.edu.au/iabusinessmanagement/SLAssessmentCriteria

Wilkes, A. (2022, Feb 7, 2022). *Internal Assessment - Business Management* . Library.scotch web site: https://library.scotch.wa.edu.au/iabusinessmanagement/HLAssessmentCriteria

PART II

SEVEN EXAMPLES OF EXCELLENT BUSINESS MANAGEMENT IA

The IA featured in this section are all recently submitted IA that scored exceptionally well (band 7) after being moderated by the IBO. The commentaries are presented in the exact same way as they were submitted, without any edits or changes to formatting. We do not retain the copyright of these IA, nor is this publication endorsed by the IBO. The Internal Assessments are being re-printed with the permission of the original authors.

1. EXAMPLE ONE (21/25)

Name: "Is Netflix in the position to invest in e-commerce merchandise?"

Author: Anonymous

Session: May 2022

Level: SL

Contents Page

Introduction

Netflix Inc. is a public limited company in which it is based on subscription streaming service which provides to its subscribers thousands of TV shows and movies ("What is Netflix?"). The company was founded in the year 1997 by two American entrepreneurs Reed Hasting and Marc Randolph. Initially, it commenced by selling DVDs, and it then changed to be a streaming service online. This had assisted them to further expand to all around America and also throughout the world and grow it's empire to what it is today (Hosch).

Throughout the years, Netflix has faced complicated limitations which are competition with other media industries such as Disney (Supporting Document 1), the obstacle of digital piracy being committed, the sharing of passwords with other users (Montefiore) and having a debt of 15 billion dollars (Supporting Document 5) clearly has affected the revenue generated by Netflix.

In order to further grow their revenue, in 2021 they have recently released their own e-commerce that sells merchandise of its popular shows called 'Netflix Shop'. With most of their subscribers at home due to the COVID pandemic, they have greatly benefitted (Supporting Document 1). Thus a question is posed and will be worthy to be investigated:

Is Netflix in the position to invest in e-commerce merchandise?

Boston Consulting Group Matrix (BCGM)

To understand whether Netflix is in the position, the analytic tools, Boston Consulting Group Matrix (BCGM) will be utilized in order to analyze the position of their products and if they will be invested in :

Table 1: BCGM of Netflix

		Market Share	
		High	Low
Market Growth	High	**Stars** Original TV Shows	**Problem Child** Netflix Shop
	Low	**Cash Cows** Streaming Other Services	**Dogs** DVD and Bluray Delivery

Based on the BCGM, Netflix Shop is a problem child. Netflix having spent less cash throughout 2020 (Supporting Document 5) has the finance to invest into Netflix Shop. As it is a problem child, building can be done with Netflix Shop in which continuous promotion will need to be done using their strong brand image for many months. Although there are risks of further finance used to promote it specially with their $15 billion debt (Supporting Document 5) in which they could use additional finance to pay their liabilities. Finance can also be obtained by milking the cash cows and using the positive cashflow to reinvest into Netflix Shop. Netflix still delivers DVDs to its customers in which they have stopped reporting the figures as they seem insignificant. With about 12 million DVDs being delivered every week (Vorel),

Netflix still can obtain profit in their strong customer loyalty in which customers are still purchasing DVDs and Blu-rays. The profit used can be invested into Netflix Shop to further expand it.

The additional finance essentially allows Netflix to be in the position to invest into Netflix Shop in which this can further help strengthen brand image and customer loyalty based on their mission statement of developing their platforms by attracting and retaining customers (Supporting Document 4). The strengthened brand image and customer loyalty, can persuade customers to purchase products in which this can further help Netflix obtain profits which can be used to reinvest into Netflix Shop to further expand and be in the position to invest.

Cash Flow Statement

Cash Flow Statement is used to estimate whether Netflix will be in the position of investing in their ecommerce. The following data is retrieved from Netflix themselves and presented through table 2 (Supporting Document 2) :

Table 2: Cash Flow Statement of Netflix ended September 30 2021

The Consolidated Cash Flow Statement (in thousands)	March 31	June 30	September 30
	Values in dollars ($)		
Net Income	1,706,715	1,353,013	1,449,071
Cash Flow from Operating Activities			
Net Cash from operating activities	777,266	(63,761)	82,379
Cash Flow From Investing Activities			
Net Cash Used in Investing	(85,616)	(111,278)	(188,631)
Cash Flow from Financing Activities			
Net Cash Used in Financing	(451,929)	(480,273)	(81,555)
Cash Flow (each month)	239,721	(655,312)	(187,807)

The Cash Flow Statement shows March having a positive cash flow of $234,721 and the months after that a negative cash flow. In 2020, the cash flow of the company was positive. However in Q2 of 2021, the cash flow had become negative. Through this the cash flow statement clearly reveals that Netflix is not currently in the position to invest in Netflix Shop.

Using a cash flow statement doesn't necessarily represent the future cash flows. Netflix Shop is currently a new product in which their mission statement of attracting and retaining customers, (Supporting Document 4) clearly makes Netflix Shop be a profitable growth towards the business, specially with how the COVID pandemic has significantly strengthened the brand image (Supporting Document 1). The strong brand image allows their customers to purchase expensive products in which massive profits can be obtained. Netflix Shop being their additional revenue stream can further generate positive cash flow in which Netflix can invest in it's ecommerce for the future. However in the future if there is still a constant negative cash flow, then the company will face liquidity problems in which they will not be able to fully invest in Netflix Shop as they will need focus more on dealing with short term debts rather then focus on their Netflix Shop, which can ultimately make Netflix not be in the position to invest in Netflix Shop. As mentioned with how cash flow was positive in 2020 due to how production was reduced, Netflix may need to look at ways to reduce production in order to improve cash flow especially with how they are stopping with external financing (Supporting Document 5). This way even if Netflix has a negative cash flow, Netflix will still be able to invest in Netflix Shop in the present and future.

Liquidity Ratio

Two Liquidity Ratios will be utilized which are Current Ratio and Acid Test (Quick) Ratio to determine the liquidity of Netflix and if they currently are in the position to pay their debts. The following formula was used (Stimpson 283 - 284):

$$Current\ Ratio = \frac{Current\ Assets}{Current\ Liability}$$

$$Acid\ Ratio = \frac{Liquid\ assets}{Current\ Liability}$$

The following data was retrieved from MicroTrends (Supporting Document 3):

Table 3: Current Ratio of Netflix Year September 2019 - 2021

Year	Current Ratio
September 2021	1.17 : 1
September 2020	1.23 : 1
September 2019	0.73 : 1

Table 4: Acid (Quick) Ratio of Netflix Year September 2019-2021

Year	Acid Ratio
September 2021	0.94 : 1
September 2020	1.05 : 1
September 2019	0.61: 1

The liquidity ratio here demonstrates Netflix having substantial liquidity. From both table 3 and 4, their current ratio and acid ratio clearly has decreased from the previous year. As mentioned with the cash flow statement, the additional revenue stream can lead to a positive cash flow in which liquidity ratios can increase in which this can make Netflix be in the position to invest even in the future. However if their liquidity still does not improve, then their problem child 'Netflix Shop' will stay as a problem child and may turn into a dog since their main issue will be to solve their liquidity problems which could make Netflix not be in the position to invest into the e-commerce. Netflix has stopped and is more focused on decreasing its debt (Lee) which leads to a clarity of Netflix improving upon their liquidity ratio slowly. Through this, Netflix essentially will be able to invest into its e-commerce merchandise.

Competition Analysis

With the evaluation of Netflix's financial situation, it is also important to analyze the e-commerce market. Netflix's idea of investing into Netflix Shop is highly competitive towards Disney. Netflix having deals with retailers like 'Target' clearly promotes Netflix Shop in which customers buy merchandise which will help increase revenue. Having a deal with retail outlets like 'Target' will also help attract new customers from Target into Netflix in which this will significantly improve profits and also persuade them to join their streaming services to also further increase revenue that can be reinvested into Netflix Shop. Their brand image and brand loyalty had been strengthened due to the pandemic, especially since Netflix has positive cash flow in 2020 (Supporting Document 5) in which Netflix is utilizing market skimming using the $135 chain and other high priced merchandise (Supporting Document 1). The high price, brand loyalty and production by well known designers, persuades customers to buy merchandise in which the high profit margin clearly provides profits in which Netflix can clearly be in the position to invest. However this can in turn make Disney or other competitors implement pricing strategies which can be used to attract more customers which can affect profit. Therefore, currently Netflix is in the position to invest in their ecommerce.

Conclusion

The BCGM reveals Netflix Shop being a problem child in which Netflix is able to invest into ecommerce based on how finance can be obtained using their cash cows. Although there is the issue of using that finance on more important things such as paying their massive debts. The Cash Flow Statement depicts Netflix in a negative cash flow since the introduction of Netflix Shop. However with the development and growth of Netflix Shop, profits will definitely arrive especially as the ecommerce is Netflix additional revenue stream. The liquidity ratio of Netflix is lower compared to previous years however they are still in the position to invest. The competition analysis reveals that to compete against Disney, Netflix has made deals with retail such as Target to increase customers. The pandemic strengthened brand loyalty and image in which Netflix is selling products at a high price. Although competitors may lower their price which may attract customers to buy from competitors. Ultimately to answer the question:

Currently, Netflix is in the position to invest in their e-commerce merchandise.

Work Cited

Hosch, William L. "Netflix." *Encyclopædia Britannica*, Encyclopædia Britannica, Inc., 9 Nov. 2020, https://www.britannica.com/topic/Netflix-Inc. Accessed: 4 August 2021

Lee, Edmund. "Netflix Will No Longer Borrow, Ending Its Run of Debt." *The New York Times*, The New York Times, 19 Jan. 2021, https://www.nytimes.com/2021/01/19/business/netflix-earnings-debt.html. Accessed: 30 December 2021

Montefiore, Abraham Sebag. "Challenges Faced by Netflix." *Medium*, Digital Society, 19 Mar. 2021, https://medium.com/digital-society/challenges-faced-by-netflix-a577e82384a. Accessed: 21 August 2021

Stimpson, Peter, and Alex Smith. *Business Management for the IB Diploma*. Second ed., Cambridge University Press, 2015.

Vorel, Jim. "The Former Netflix DVD Library Is a Lost Treasure We'll Never See Again." *Pastemagazine.com*, Paste Magazine, 23 Mar. 2021, https://www.pastemagazine.com//netflix-dvd-service-plan-subscribers-/. Accessed: 30 December 2021

2. EXAMPLE TWO (24/25)

Name: '"Which products should Hoa Phuong Tourism Joint Stock Company develop to attract existing markets?"

Author: Anonymous

Session: May 2022

Level: HL

1. RESEARCH QUESTION:

"Which products should Hoa Phuong Tourism Joint Stock Company develop to attract existing markets?"

2. PROPOSED METHODOLOGY:

2.1. The rationale for study:

Hoa Phuong Tourism Joint Stock Company offers vacation packages for high-income households and large-group tourists in Hai Phong. During the Covid-19 epidemic, the business realizes the recent changes in travel habits as followings:

- An ever-blooming number of independent travelers and small group tourists due to Covid-19 concerns.
- A rising demand for travel products featuring less-crowded destinations, new-brand outings, and discounted prices.

The director opines that this trend will continue at least the first few years after the post-epidemic. Consequently, he aims to develop new products to appeal to existing markets, resulting in improving profitability.

2.2. Areas of the syllabus to be covered:

4.2. Market segmentation – Segmenting the company's markets to differentiate its services by building distinctive customer profiles.

4.4. Primary market research – Gathering first-hand data from the company's customers to understand how their travel habits have changed during the epidemic and what would make them repurchase services from the company.

4.4. Secondary market research – Gathering second-hand data to understand the outlook for Vietnamese tourism post-pandemic and customers' travel habits.

4.4. Qualitative and quantitative research – Qualitative analysis aims to gain In-depth understanding of customers' travel habits. Quantitative analysis is used in primary and secondary research to understand the quantitative characteristics of market segments, such as their income or allocation of budgets for traveling.

4.4. Sampling – Finding the appropriate sampling to avoid bias or inadequate sample size, hence increasing the validity of the results.

2.3. Possible sources of information:

	Organizations and individuals to be approached:	*Methods to be used to collect and analyze data, and the reason for choosing them:*	
Primary sources:	HPTJSC's director	Interview	The current-serving markets, travel products, and the aims of the company.
	HPTJSC's customers	Survey	The reason for changing travel habits of the customers.
	5 HR Managers from 5 large companies in Hai Phong	Interview	Travel habits of companies in Hai Phong.
Secondary sources:	Cimigo, VNexpress, IndoChina Capital	Reports related to the travel habits in Vietnam's domestic tourism.	Gain a basis of knowledge about travel habits and find the gaps that require data to understand the research question.

3. ANTICIPATED DIFFICULTIES:

3.1. Limited information obtained from first-hand data.

Focus more on qualitative analysis such as giving more open questions to increase the quality of responses.

3.2. Differences between business concepts coined by Vietnamese and English.

Consulting with Vietnamese businessmen and overseas Vietnamese business students to understand Vietnamese business terminology, hence minimizing misunderstandings with the director and HR managers.

4. ACTION PLAN:

Date	Action	Sources	Anticipated Difficulties	Modifications
August 28th	1st draft's IA Research Proposal.	-	Edit accordingly supervisor's suggestions.	Narrow down the research question's topic.
September 15th	Interview questions with director and 5 HR managers of	-	-	Schedule interviews with the director and 5

	large businesses. Survey for the company's customers.			HR managers.
September 19th	Conduct interviews and survey	Director, customers, HR managers.	-	-
September 21st	Collect Secondary data.	-	-	-
October 25th	Finalize primary research's data.	-	-	-
October 8th	First Draft's IA			
October 15th	Edit accordingly supervisor's suggestions.	-	-	-
November 27th	Finalize & format document.	-	-	-
December 13th	Final Draft of IA Business Management			

CONTENTS PAGE:

1. EXECUTIVE SUMMARY:

During the Covid-19 pandemic, customers have changed their travel habits. Recognizing that, the executive director considers resegmenting existing markets to better serve his customers by building distinct consumer profiles and diversifying into new products if needed.

Market segmentation and product development could help the company remain competitive and improve profitability, hence the question: "Which products should Hoa Phuong Tourism Joint Stock Company develop to attract existing markets?"

Collecting secondary data to determine missing information that is needed to answer the research question and to provide a better primary research.

Conducting primary research as followings:

- A survey with the company's customers: Understand the existing customers' travel habits and desirable products.
- Interviews with five HR Managers from five Haiphong's companies: Understanding the local business customers' travel habits.
- Weekly interviews with the director: Understanding about the company's existing markets, current products, and reasons for market segmentation and product development.

Thirdly, I resegment the existing markets based on age, current occupation and position, income, marital status, etc.

2. INTRODUCTION:

Hoa Phuong Tourism is a private limited tour-operating company that offers luxurious packages for high-income households and large businesses in Hai Phong. Its customers prefer services as follows: high-end resorts, exclusive buffets, and recreational activities.

As the Covid-19 pandemic has changed customers' travel habits, the director believes that concentrating on existing markets could help the company remain competitive and maximize profitability in the short term. Therefore, the director considers market segmentation and product development to achieve the aforementioned objectives

3. RESEARCH QUESTION:

Which products should Hoa Phuong Tourism Joint Stock Company develop to attract existing markets?

4. METHODOLOGY EMPLOYED:

This research uses three primary and three secondary sources to generate well-advised research.

4.1. Primary sources:

4.1.1. Weekly interviews with the director: understanding about the company's existing markets, services, and reasons for market segmentation and product development.

4.1.2. Qualitative interview with five HR managers from five companies in Hai Phong: Understanding customers in existing markets that have not used the company's services before.

For instance, knowing about their taste and preferences could help the company determine which products they should develop accordingly, hence maximizing the existing markets.

Since HR managers take responsibility for companies' trips, they tend to book tours for their families from the tour operators who organize trips for their companies, hence making HR managers fit into the existing markets of the Hoa Phuong Tourism.

Snowballing is used to determine the sample based on the researcher's mother's network as she is a HR manager. It is not recommended to use the director's network as his partners might respond biasedly to avoid weakening relationships with the director.

4.1.3. Quantitative survey with the company's customers: Understanding the existing customers' travel habits, and products the company should offer to increase customer satisfaction and loyalty.

Random Sampling is used to collect responses as the existing markets have very similar characteristics based on their ages, income, marital status, tastes and preferences.

4.2. Secondary sources:

Three secondary sources from Cimigo, VNexpress, and IndoChinaCapital are to gain knowledge about travel habits of Vietnamese customers from recent reports, hence determining gaps that require answering the research question and also providing a well-advised primary research.

5. MAIN RESULTS AND FINDINGS:

The quantitative survey reveals:

There are 42.8% respondents aged between 25 and 34, followed by 38.16% people in the age range from 35 to 44. Regarding current occupation, 61.9% people acquire full-time jobs while that for houseworkers account for 19.04%. Following that, 71.4% respondents are managers in corporations while 23.8% are unemployed. In terms of income, 47.6% households receive high monthly salaries, ranging from 30 to 40 million VND. Dominating the figure for marital status is married, accounting for 33.3%. According to respondents, they prefer to try local food, relax and experience services at luxurious resorts, and attend cultural events and festivals. Additionally, respondents travel to take beautiful pictures taking the lion's share of 33.3%. The criteria when planning a trip are prioritized as discounted packages with high value, recreational activities, and opportunities for taking photos.

The qualitative interview reveals:

When asking about the HR managers' priorities when organizing a tour for their company, five people prefer safety and avoid crowded destinations. Three managers are interested in discounted packages with greater value perceived.

When asking if the respondents continue to consume travel products provided by the tour operator of their companies, three people vote yes, one is neutral, and one votes no.

6. ANALYSIS AND EVALUATION:

6.1. Primary Quantitative Market Research:

The survey was conducted with the participation of 21 customers who have used the company's services before.

Question 1: Which range do you age fit into?

	Number	Percentages (%)
25 - 34	9	42.80
35 - 44	8	38.16
45 - 54	4	19.04
54+	0	0.00

Table 1. Age groups of customers participating in the survey.

Question 2: What is your current occupation?

	Number	Percentage (%)
Full-time jobs (More than 40 hours per week)	13	61.90
Part-time jobs (Less than 40 hours per week)	1	5.06
Housewife/Househusband	4	19.04

Unemployed	3	14.00

Table 2. Current occupations of customers participating in the survey.

Question 3: What is your current occupation's level?

	Number	Percentage (%)
Unemployed	5	23.80
Intern	0	0.00
Officer	1	4.80
Manager	15	71.40

Table 3. Current employment positions of customers participating in the survey.

Question 4: What is your monthly household income regarding VND currency?

	Number	Percentage (%)
Below 9,999,999 VND.	1	4.78
10,000,000 - 19,999,999 VND.	1	4.78
20,000,000 - 29,999,999 VND.	5	23.80
30,000,000 - 39,999,999 VND.	10	47.60
40,000,000 - 49,999,999 VND.	4	19.04

Table 4. Monthly household income of customers participating in the survey (VND).

Question 5: What is your marital status?

	Number	Percentage (%)
Single	5	23.80
Married	7	33.30
In a relationship.	5	23.80
Preferred not to answer.	4	19.10

Table 5. Marital status of customers participating in the survey.

Question 6: What are your preferred activities? (You might pick more than one).

	Number	Percentage (%) out of 21 respondents
Doing recreational activities at beaches	5	23.80
Relaxing and experiencing services at resorts.	7	33.30
Trying local food	10	47.60
Visiting religious sites, museums, and historical sites.	2	9.50
Visiting amusement parks, safares, and other entertaining sites.	5	23.80
Attending cultural events and festivals.	7	33.33

Table 6. Activities preferred by customers participating in the survey.

Question 7: What is your purpose of travelling?

	Number	Percentage (%)
Relax and relieve stress.	5	23.81
Spend quality time with family and friends.	1	4.76
Discover new things.	3	14.29
Have fun and excitement.	5	23.81
Take beautiful pictures.	7	33.33

Table 7. Travel purpose of customers participating in the survey.

Question 8: What are your criteria when organizing a trip? (You might pick more than one).

	Number	Percentage (%)
Beautiful landscapes.	5	23.81
Nice climate.	4	19.05
Less-crowded destinations.	7	33.30
Discounted packages with high value.	15	71.43
Opportunities for taking photos.	10	47.62
Recreational activities.	12	57.14

Table 8. Criteria of customers when organizing a trip.

6.2. Primary Qualitative Market Research:

The interview was conducted with five HR Managers from Ecoba Vietnam Joint Stock Company, LSVina-Cable System Joint Stock Company, Vico Vietnam Co., Ltd, Vietnam Marine University, and Bee Logistics Corporation.

The answers were shortened to feature the main point of the responses.

Question 1: What do you prioritize when organizing a tour for your company?

	Number	Percentage (%) out of 5 respondents.
Safety	4	80.00
Discounted Prices	3	60.00
Recreational Activities	2	40.00
E-Booking	1	20.00

Table 9. Priority of HR managers when organizing a company's tour.

Question 2: Do you think you will book tours for your family from the tour operator that design tours for your company?

	Number	Percentage (%)
Yes	3	60.00
No	1	20.00
Neutral	1	20.00

Table 10. Managers' responses to as whether they would book family tours from the tour operator who design tours for their companies.

6.3. Market Segmentation:

Based on the quantitative survey, market segmentation was conducted to build distinct consumer profiles, hence providing an insight into the products that are in the best interest of the existing markets. Eight factors based on demographic, psychographic, and behavioral are listed as followings: age, current occupation, employment position, marital status, household income, preferred activities, travel purpose, and criterion when planning a trip. The qualitative interview also helps to determine the firmographic for the market segment of business customers.

Figure 11. Market segmentation based on the primary research.

<table>
<tr><td colspan="6">Age</td></tr>
<tr><td colspan="2">25 - 34</td><td colspan="2">35 - 44</td><td colspan="2">45 - 54</td></tr>
<tr><td colspan="6">Current Occupation</td></tr>
<tr><td colspan="3">Full-time jobs</td><td colspan="3">Housewife/Househusband</td></tr>
<tr><td colspan="6">Employment Position</td></tr>
<tr><td colspan="3">Manager</td><td colspan="3">Unemployed</td></tr>
<tr><td colspan="6">Marital Status</td></tr>
<tr><td colspan="2">Married</td><td colspan="2">Single</td><td colspan="2">In a relationship</td></tr>
<tr><td colspan="6">Household Income</td></tr>
<tr><td colspan="3">Middle Income: 20,000,000 - 29,999,999 VND</td><td colspan="3">High Income: 30,000,000 VND - 49,999,999 VND</td></tr>
<tr><td colspan="6">Preferred Activities:</td></tr>
<tr><td>Trying local food</td><td>Attending cultural events</td><td>Relaxing and experiencing at resorts</td><td colspan="2">Visiting amusement parks, safaris, and other entertaining sites.</td><td>Doing recreational activities at beaches.</td></tr>
<tr><td colspan="6">Travel Purpose</td></tr>
<tr><td colspan="2">Taking beautiful pictures.</td><td colspan="2">Relaxing and relieving stress.</td><td colspan="2">Having fun and excitement.</td></tr>
<tr><td colspan="6">Criterion for a tour</td></tr>
<tr><td colspan="2">Discounted packages with high values</td><td colspan="2">Opportunities for taking photos</td><td>Safety measures</td><td>Recreational activities</td></tr>
</table>

Initially, the director identifies that there are two market segments: high-income households and large businesses with one available premium package that features relaxing and experiencing services at luxurious resorts.

However, after resegmenting the existing markets, the results turn out to be an unidentified niche market for middle-income households that earn from 20 million to under 30 million VND. Also, the existing markets appear to have unmet demand for preferred activities listed as trying local food; attending cultural events and festivals; visiting amusement parks, safaris; and other entertaining sites; and doing recreational activities at beaches. Since the company only specializes in providing luxurious services at resorts and ignores other unmet needs of the existing customers, this could result in a loss of customers and barriers to expand its customer base in the long term. Given the fact that the travel habits have been changing, the demand for relaxing services at premium resorts only accounts for 33.33%, among other preferences.

Furthermore, the firmographic segmentation based on the qualitative interview reveals that the concerns about safety and hygiene measures and risks of Covid-19 infections have been rising among businesses. As a matter of fact, several Covid-19 outbreaks in Vietnam were caused by crowded destinations and travelling in large groups of tourists. Hence, this further explains why HR managers are concerned about the travel products featuring wellness, authenticity, and safety. Also, Covid-19 pandemic has plugged Vietnam's economy, weakening the financial positions of the majority of businesses. More precisely, businesses have to shut down, meaning loss of revenues and profits whereas they still have to pay fixed costs such as maintenance costs of machinery or rental costs. Thus, in reopening the economy, more businesses demand for discounted packages with greater value to offer vacation tours for their employees as a reward (MICE).

Lastly, recreational activities have been demanded by both existing customers of the company (57.14%) and HR managers (2 out of 5). Regarding households, as nationwide lockdown has created social distancing between family members, participating in recreational activities during a trip could strengthen the bonds of the families. In respect of businesses, the anti-virus policy also made workforce work from home, creating distance between managers and workers. Such aforementioned activities could form a stronger bonding between employees and employers, as employees feel that they are rewarded for their hard work during the epidemic.

6.4. Product Development:

To spread risks by diversifying into new products, given the context of changing customers' tastes and preferences, Hoa Phuong Tourism could provide two new travel products -- food tourism and MICE tourism and tailor its current product -- premium leisure tourism to better serve its existing markets.

6.4.1. Gastronomy tourism:

Gastronomy tourism provides customers with experiencing local culinary specialities, learning how to cook local recipes, attending local fairs and festivals to learn about local culture, and taking beautiful pictures with food and festivals. Also, gastronomy tourism could serve the middle-income segment since the tour package only lasts for one to two days which is relatively affordable for this market segment. Also, gastronomy tourism could be viewed as a rarely-exploited niche market if the company organizes tours in Northern Vietnam. This is because tour operators mainly design tours in Central Vietnam where they offer national heritages and landscapes while ignoring the fact that Northern Vietnam such as Hai Phong offers a rich culture of cuisine. Organizing gastronomy tours in Haiphong could also be advantageous for the business since it is based in Haiphong, hence having a solid knowledge of local markets and cultures.

6.4.2. MICE Tourism:

Hoa Phuong tourism could combine MICE Tourism with Premium Leisure Tourism to meet the demand for business customers. This is because such customers desire recreational activities for discounted prices with high value. The "I" component in MICE refers to Incentives, that is, trips offered by companies to reward their employees for their hard work or progress. The tour operator could practice with the "I" component first to see how the existing markets would react to the travel products, hence better tailoring their services. This development could be perceived as a less-risk growth strategy since the company has previous experience in serving premium leisure tourism, combining with recreational activities would only require training sources for the company's tourist guides, for instance.

Furthermore, concentrating on existing markets would help the company increase customer loyalty. According to the qualitative responses, 3 out of 5 HR managers say that they will continue to book family tours from the company as they would benefit from the exclusive promotions. One respondent says that she would consider purchasing travel products for families if the company offers discounted prices for small tour packages.

7. CONCLUSIONS AND RECOMMENDATIONS:

7.1. Conclusions:

In general, diversifying into new travel packages listed as Gastronomy Tourism and MICE tourism appear to be potential for the company to meet its existing markets. The results and analysis also reveal that the product development is a low-risk growth strategy for the business. Both qualitative and quantitative research reveal the changes in existing markets' tastes and preferences.

7.2. Limitations:

However, the snowball sampling still contains the possibility of biased responses despite using the researcher's mother's network. Also, the size of the sample for both quantitative and qualitative analysis is relatively small due to the time constraints and difficulties to identify the population.

7.3. Recommendations:

It is recommended that the director should conduct further research to understand the market segment using more unbiased sampling methods such as cluster or random sampling with a larger sample size to obtain better results.

Also, the director could conduct perception maps to see how his services are perceived by the customers. This method also helps the company identify gaps in the market segments.

BIBLIOGRAPHY + APPENDICES OMITTED

3. EXAMPLE THREE (23/25)

Name: 'Should Fighting Fit Club and British International School Istanbul re-establish a concession as a growth strategy?'

Author: Anonymous

Session: May 2021

Level: HL

1 Research Proposal

1.1 Research Question

Should Fighting Fit Club and and British International School Istanbul re-establish a concession as a growth strategy?

1.2 Rationale

Fighting Fit Club (FFC) is service business with a new facility found in Istanbul, Sarıyer. Convienitely, its location is near British International School Istanbul (BISI). It is around 5 kilometers way, that is, a 10 minute drive. A recent survey conducted by the school suggests that parents are most unsatisfied with the Physical Education provided by the school in comparison to other subjects (66 respondents).

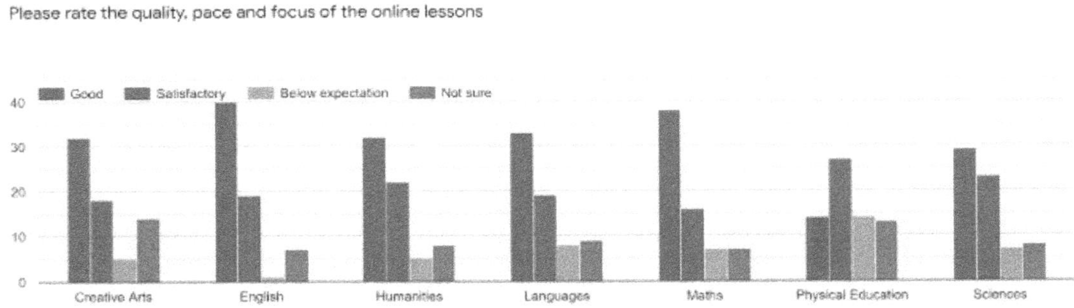

Figure 1: Survey result for the question "Please rate the quality, pace and focus of the online lessons" (Robinson, 2020)

Evidently, maintaining a healthy lifestyle was shown to be a challenge for the vast majority (that is, students, staff and parents) because of the strict lock downs announced by the government. Today, these restrictions are less strict and selective groups are being called to school physically. Moreover, given that FFC and BISI have already established a very short concession pre-pandemic which was mainly targetted to students, this may be shown beneficial for both businesses to see whether such a concession is possible again, however, now taking account new specialised features such as newly offered sports, new target markets (parents and staff) and new safety measurements.

1.3 Questionnaire/Survey/Interview Audience and Plan

People/Organisation	Reason
CEO/Employee of FFC	Inflict opinion on such a possible concession. Does the current research link with the objectives of FFC?
Head of PE Department (Christian Huegel)	His opinion on how positively and negatively such a concession might affect the PE Department, the objectives of the PE Department
Students	Their opinion as the main customer base on an access to a premium gym
Head of Secondary (Richard Robinson)	His opinion on how such a concession would affect the school's image, whether it meets the school's objectives

Table 1: Group of people that will be interviewed and/or be surveyed

1.4 Areas of Syllabus Covered

1.3 Organisational Objectives

4.2 Marketing Planning

4.4 Market Research

4.5 4Ps - Price, Place, Product, Promotion

1.5 Primary Research

- Interview with the CEO or an employee of Fighting Fit Club
- Questionnaire for students from years 7-13
- Interview with the Head of Secondary
- Interview with the Head of PE Department

1.6 Secondary Research

- Fighting Fit Club Website - Mission and Vision statements, objectives, sources for contacting
- MACFit Website - Information for availability, type of sports
- Cambridge Business Management Textbook - tools, information

- British International School Website - Mission and Vision statements, objectives

1.7 Possible Difficulties

Possible Problems	Possible Solutions
The CEO of Fighting Fit Club or employee might not disclose the information that I am seeking	Other factors will be considered when making the decision
The CEO of Fighting Fit Club or employee might have a busy schedule, thus I might not be able to interview them	A scheduled time is necessary through phone, email etc. to guarantee a place or a spot and time to speak and disclose the information required
Not enough answers for the PE Questionnaire	Ask teachers to inform about the questionnaire and add it to the weekly bulletin to raise awareness

Table 2: Possible problems and solutions

1.8 Action plan

Unfortunately, due to COVID-19, the original plan and Gantt chart was delayed by a large amount, with a huge break between February and October. Therefore, there are 2 Gantt charts, one for which is initial (January-February) and the later (October-December) to show reflect upon these modifications.

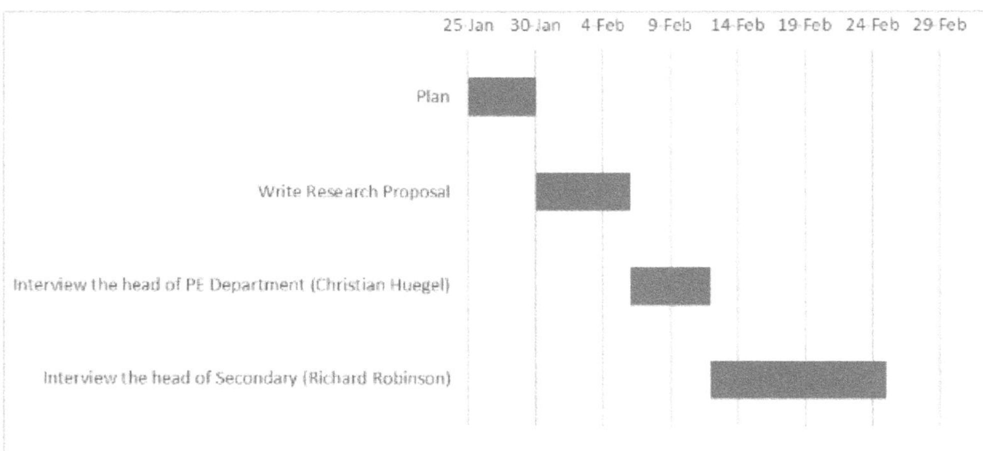

Figure 2: (Part 1 of 2) Gantt chart from January to February

Contents

2 Written Report

2.1 Executive Summary

The Fighting Fit Club (FFC) used to be in a concession with British International School Istanbul (BISI), until the COVID-19 outbreak set curfews and lock downs. However, this has been seen as a possible opportunity that FFC can take due to the declining quality of fitness and health of individuals. This lead to the research question "Should Fighting Fit Club and British International School Istanbul re-establish a concession as a growth strategy?"

Primary research was conducted using interviews with various notable employees of both businesses. An interview was sent out to parents and students to further investigate sports interests of potential customers. Multiple different possibilities of re-concession were taken into account: in gym during class, in school during class or out of school clubs. To analyse and optimise the concession the 4Ps, BCG Matrix, and the product positioning map were used.

In conclusion, both the school and FFC can benefit from each other. The FFC should re-establish a concession with the school by introducing after school clubs by prioritising Pilates, Tang Soo Do and Cross Body fit in ranked order. Lastly, it is worth considering to introduce a new sport which can appeal to the old and masculine market.

2.2 Introduction

Fighting Fit Club (FFC) is a newly established (2012) sole-trader sports complex business with three sports halls located in various provinces of Turkey. The FFC Istanbul sports hall is conveniently located next to an International school, giving various opportunities for FFC to establish concessions. Before the pandemic, FFC offered lessons of Tang Soo Do, Fitness and Functional Training inside the school in after school sessions, most of which were targeted at the students, teachers and the parents of the students. However, due to the COVID-19 pandemic, lock downs and curfews were initiated which resulted in the end of the concession between the school and FFC. On the contrary, the end of the concession may also be a beginning of an opportunity: with the increasing lock downs and curfews, individual fitness and health has become a topic of everyone's concern. This became further evident with the results of the school's Physical Education quality. Hence, this Internal Assessment will explore whether a re-concession would be advantageous for both sides by confirming the organisational objectives of both businesses, and how the FFC should ultimately be re-introduced to the school to effectively stimulate FFC's growth and gain an advantage against its competitor MACFit.

2.3 Research Question

Should Fighting Fit Club and British International School Istanbul re-establish a concession as a growth strategy?

2.4 Methodology Employed

A total of four primary researches were conducted for this Internal Assessment. Three of these were interviews, one was an online questionnaire sent out to the students. The aim of the interviews was to get detailed answers in regards to sustained values of the businesses, their opinion on each others' businesses, and opinion with regards to several possibilities of a re-concession (e.g. through integration of FFC in PE lessons in school, or in FFC's sports hall with their equipment, or after school). The online questionnaire was aimed to extract students' and parents' interest and opinion on various possible sports, individual availability and safety concerns due to COVID-19.

2.5 Main Results and Findings

2.5.1 Christian Huegel Interview

[1]The consent for the recording of the transcript was asked. Moreover, the interview was conducted before COVID-19, hence some unnecessary information for the IA such as the the "Year 10 program" can be found in the transcript. The main results of the interview, however, can be shortened as follows:

- Believes that the current equipment of the school is sufficient.
- Is happy with Fighting Fit Club's presence, was used by some teachers and students for fitness previously.
- Having concessions to replace PE lessons is not financially solvable by the school.
- However, a PE lesson concession during winter might be an opportunity because outdoor gyms cannot be used, meaning that they're lacking space.

2.5.2 Richard Robinson Interview

[2]The consent for the recording of the transcript was asked. Moreover, the interview was conducted before COVID-19, hence some unnecessary information for the IA such as the the "Year 10 program" can be found in the transcript. The main results of the interview, however, can be shortened as follows:

- The director, Richard Robinson, focuses on the improvement of the PE department with continuous improvement.
- The current PE department lacks space, and more PE equipment for lessons is always welcome.
- Bringing students to the gym of FFC might be troublesome due to dangers of walking across road and can be costly using school bus
- A concession would fit the objectives of the school by promoting health and fitness

2.5.3 FFC Employee Interview

[3]The consent for the recording of the transcript was asked, however, the permission was denied. Hence, summary to the questions asked were written in real time instead. The main results of the interview can be shortened as follows:

- FFC having concessions with other schools has been done before in Izmir.
- The business's mission and vision statement fits with Richard Robinson's mission and vision statement, that is to promote health.
- Would like to work with BISI again, has had experience with working in BISI
- The busiest times of the business include Mondays, Tuesdays, Thursdays and Fridays, when group lessons are offered.

2.5.4 Questionnaire Results

The student questionnaire was created using Google Forms [4]. Because the interviews proved that having in-school lessons with the FFC is difficult, the questionnaire aimed to see whether a concession as an after

[2]See Appendix B for the transcript
[3]See Appendix C for the interview summary
[4]The questions can be found in Appendix D

school club for both parents and students is possible. Hence, it was aimed to see whether potential customers would be satisfied with such a concession.

This graph shows whether the respondents would attend sports lessons with trained professionals in consideration with social distancing measures in school

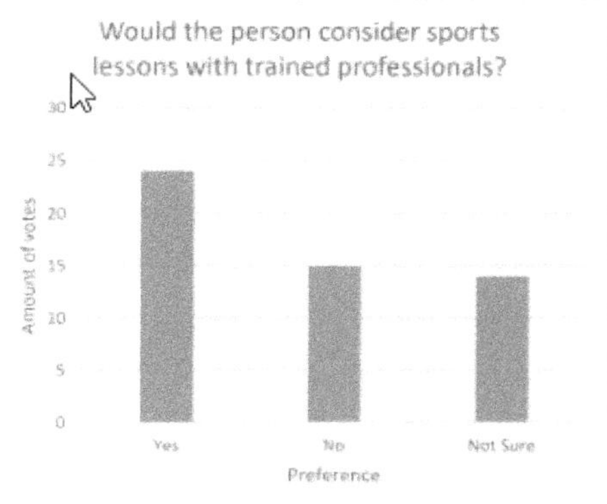

Figure 1: Would the person consider sports lessons with trained professionals?

This graph shows the days at which the respondents were most comfortable in attending the lessons on. The most popular choice was Wednesday, followed closely by Monday.

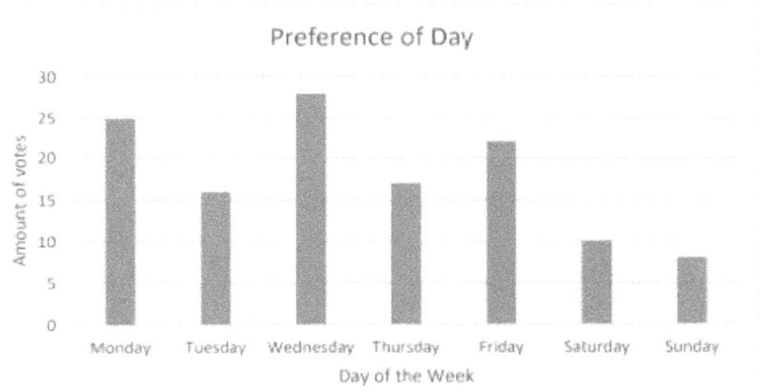

Figure 2: Preference of day

This graph shows the times at which the respondents were most comfortable in attending the lessons on. The time range of 15:00-16:30 was the most preferred. Similarly, 16:30-18:00 was the second most popu-

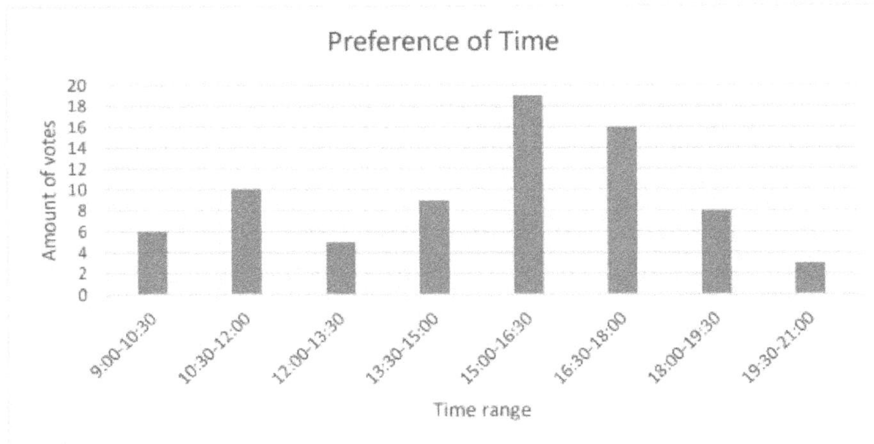

Figure 3: Preference of time

This graph shows the results of the questionnaire, for which was aimed at parents and students of the school. In the result below, the word "adult" is defined to be respondents who are at the age of 19+. Students were excluded in these results due to their dependency in finance and costs, even if their results were collected. The graph below shows that the most preferred cost range is 800 – 1000 TL.

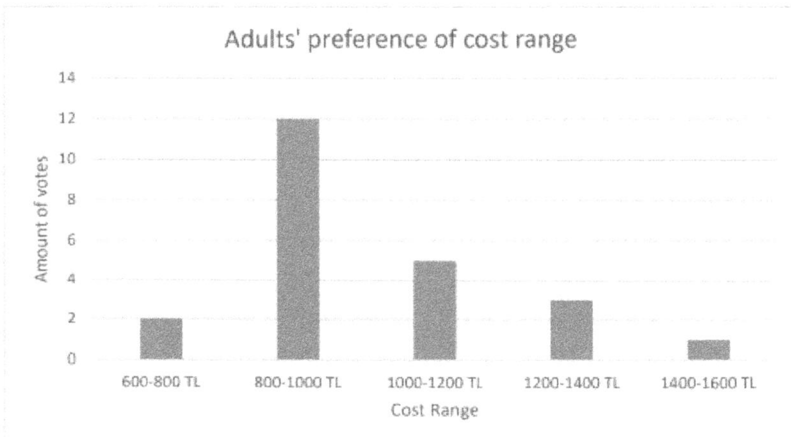

Figure 4: Adults' preference of cost range

This graph shows the relationship between age and sports preferences listed in the questionnaire. Kickboxing especially attracted younger individuals. Pilates, on the other hand, was preferred the most by older individuals. One person was also excluded from the results as they did not want to disclose their age.

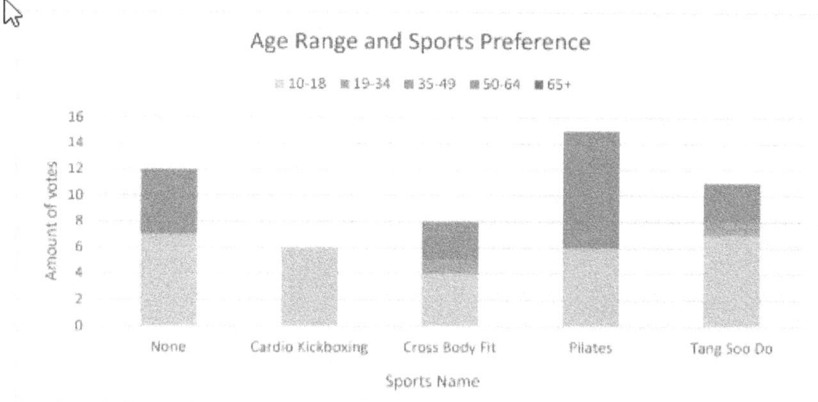

Figure 5: Age range and sports preference

This graph shows the relationship between gender and sports preferences listed in the questionnaire. Pilates was the most liked sports by the majority, with this majority mostly being female.

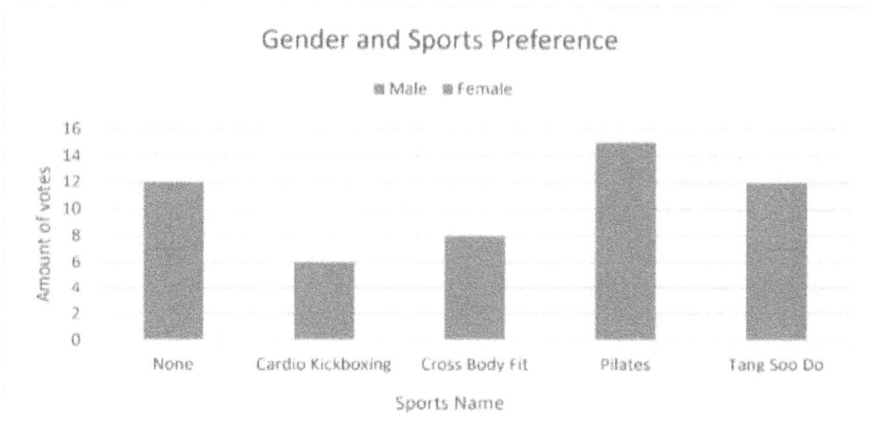

Figure 6: Gender and sports preference

2.6 Analysis and Discussion

2.6.1 Overview

Because the majority of people have chosen most popular time range to be within 15:00-16:30 and 16:30-18:00, the following analysis will be based upon the idea of implementing a concession using the school's gym and the FFC's own equipment for the private lessons as an after school club. The most safest COVID-19 area in the school is the outdoor football field due to the natural ventilation and large area for social distancing. It can approximately hold 60 customers.

2.6.2 Product Positioning Map

We will use the product positioning in an attempt to answer why a high portion of the respondents (22.6%) responded none, to find which audience FFC may be failing to appeal, if any.

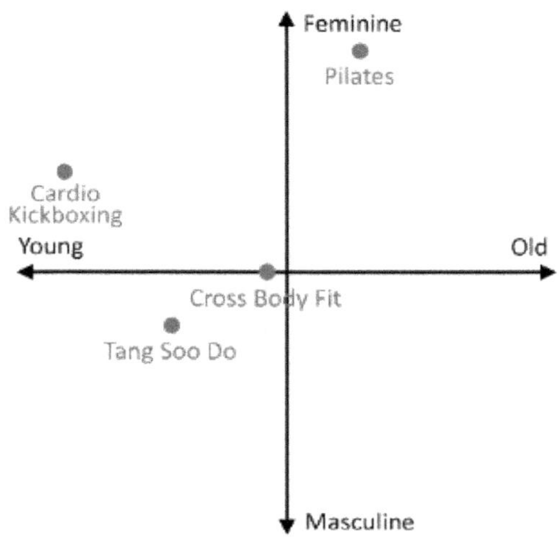

Figure 7: The product positioning map from survey results

After positioning from survey results, a lack of "masculine" and "old" sports is evidently missing. The introduction of a sport which can fit within the category of "old" and "masculine" can help gaining the missing potential customers. Moreover, from the statistics, the large portion of respondents who responded "None" are respondents are also mostly male and old, coinciding with our mapping. Hence we are looking for a new sport which can theoretically fit the following:

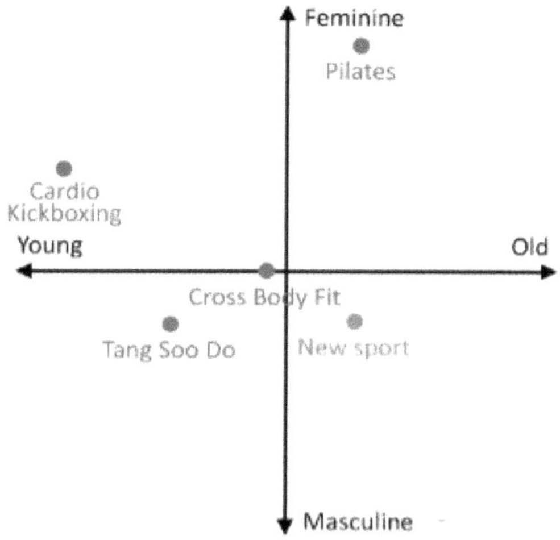

Figure 8: The product positioning map with the "new" sport

For which can result in a more possible successful concession between the FFC and the school, as it allows to cover a broader market.

2.6.3 Boston Consulting Group Matrix

The BCG matrix is a tool used for businesses to help decide which products or services are worth for further investment, allowing to plan future strategies (Stimpson & Smith, 2005, p.402). The BCG Matrix was constructed using local knowledge, information of available sports from competitor's website (*MACFit Ormanada*, 2021) in local region, and survey results.

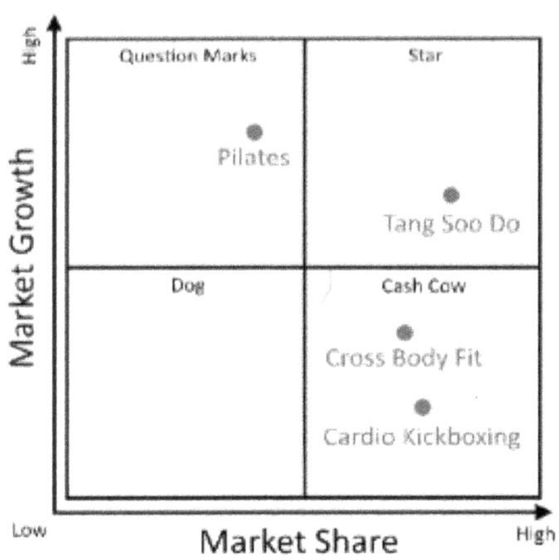

Figure 9: BCG Matrix for the sports

With pilates placed as a question mark as a result of high availability of the sport in the local MACFit gym, a concession with the school can ultimately increase the market share. This implies that there is potential for the sport to move onto the "Star" category, potentially increasing the revenue generated.

2.6.4 Marketing Mix

The purpose of the marketing mix is to find the right combination P's so FFC can gain and maintain advantage over MACFit in the concession (Lumen, n.d.). All price calculations will be done taking the samples from the survey of 53 respondents (9.8% response rate) and extrapolating them to a larger population. With the approximation of 181 secondary students and hence approximately 362 parents, there are 543 potential customers. Through survey results, extrapolating the result in Figure 1 yields us 246 potential customers.

2.6.4.1 Price

i	**Price Range (TL)**	**% of adults who are willing to pay equal range or higher (x_i) (3 significant figures)**	**Approximate amount of customers (y_i) ($y_i = 246 \times \frac{x_i}{100}$) (rounded to the nearest whole number)**	**Potential Revenue (z_i) (z_i = Mean price range $\times y_i$) (TL)**	**Potential Revenue with the limit of the football field (60 people or less) (TL)**
1	600-800	100	246	172200	42000
2	800-1000	91.3	225	202500	54000
3	1000-1200	39.1	96	105600	66000
4	1200-1400	17.4	43	55900	55900
5	1400-1600	4.35	11	16500	16500

A 3 month revenue forecast suggests that the most profitable price range that FFC should choose is 1000 – 1200 TL, which brings in the most revenue out of all using the statistics from our survey. Hence, no pricing techniques such as pricing discrimination is required, as the range falls well within the business's current prices and is optimised for the concession.

2.6.4.2 Place

The location of the concession is the school. That is, from results in interviews with Christian Huegel and Richard Robinson who have highlighted that transportation, cost etc. to the gym of FFC is inconvenient, hence it is appropriate to offer lessons in the school. This option is convenient for FFC since the distance of both businesses is minimal. The most popular time ranges coincide with the time the school finishes (15:30), hence it is appropriate to hold lessons after school. This is also convenient for the customers, as students and parents who pick up their children are given the option to attend lessons immediately after regular lessons. Lastly, the school is also in close proximity to MACFit Ormanada ($\approx 100m$) which can in turn aid FFC to gain market share in the relative area.

2.6.4.3 Product

FFC's branding is designed to be viewed as high quality, hence the premium price. This makes stand out in comparison to MACFit, a generic chain of sports gyms and lessons, differentiating its services. The service offered by FFC clearly satisfies the created demand of a healthy lifestyle as seen in Figure 1.

2.6.4.4 Promotion

The promotion of the concession is not relatively required, which can save costs. Given that the reputation of FFC is held well within Richard Robinson and Christian Huegel, it is implied that FFC's reputation in school is well established among staff, which can extrapolate further into parents and students. Furthermore, promotion, although unnecessary, could be established in school at relatively no cost. This could be advertising through in-school posters, school weekly bulletins. In fact, the survey that was shared with students and parents is in a sense also advertisement suggesting of a possible re-concession.

2.7 Conclusion

- A re-concession by utilising real time lessons of the school is inconvenient for the school.
- Both businesses overlap in their mission and vision statements with positive feedback from school staff, and thus a re-concession is likely.
- The concession may help the students' and parents' satisfaction with sports of the school, given that a large majority would consider attending professional lessons.
- There is a high demand for sports due to the declining fitness of individuals as a result of the pandemic, which is reflected within the surveys and is an advantage the FFC can take.
- There is a lack of an "old-masculine" sport which is causing a loss of potential customers and thus sales for the FFC.
- Pilates is a sport which can be considerably benefited with market share due to the concession, potentially making it a star.

- The price set by the FFC is appropriate and does not require any discriminatory pricing specific for the concession.

2.8 Recommendation

- The FFC should look into having a concession with the school to take advantage of the COVID-19 pandemic. Both businesses can ultimately prove useful for each other.
- This concession should not consist of offering alternative PE lessons to students during classes
- This concession instead should consist of lessons offered after school, and should mainly focus on Pilates, Tang Soo Do and Cross Body Fit.
- The FFC should not change the price of their products
- The FFC should should introduce a sport which can appeal to the old and masculine market

2.9 Limitations

- The total amount of respondents for the survey was low (53). More responses would yield to more accurate results.
- It is possible that the audience which answered the questionnaire are more enthusiastic about sports as a result of selective bias when choosing to answer. Hence, the uninterested population may be underrepresented.
- The statistical market share of FFC and its competitors is not known, hence judgment was used using local knowledge. Having statistical data of the market share would help for more accurate analysis.

BIBLIOGRAPHY + APPENDICES OMITTED

4. EXAMPLE FOUR (24/25)

Name: 'Should Flabeg invest into industrial robots to increase profitability?

Author: Anonymous

Session: May 2021

Level: HL

Research Proposal

Research Question

Should Flabeg invest into industrial robots to increase profitability?

Rationale

Flabeg is a private limited company (Ltd) that provides automotive businesses with car mirrors, as well as manufactures internal, external sun visors, and cover glass for displays. The objective of this firm is to be the global leader in providing glass and mirror components for automotive companies. Since it is a Ltd, the biggest aim is to gain profits. Flabeg has identified two problems that disallow them from increasing profitability; 1. not being able to enter new markets, which have mainly low-cost car models, 2. struggling with high unit costs due to high labor costs as well as too high defect rate. Due to high unit costs, the firm has low competitiveness, and the Flabeg management's solution is to reduce direct labor costs by robotization of various production processes, hopefully increasing the output quality rate and productivity.

Theoretical Framework

Syllabus	Tool	Justification
1.7 Organizational Objectives	SWOT	Examines the current situation, therefore provides context to look at the current strengths and weaknesses

		(firm's high unit costs) and opportunities and threats (potential reduced demand).
1.7 Organizational Planning Tools	Force Field analysis (FFA)	Identifies the pressures for and pressures against a decision or a change.
3.8 Investment Appraisal	Net Present Value (NPV)	Calculates the total value of future stream of payments.
5.5 Production Planning	- Capacity utilization rate	Used to investigate whether or not the production line is fully utilized (investment justification)
	- Productivity rate	Comparing the productivity rate of the personnel (direct labor) and industrial robot.

Most of these do not detail why they answer the question.
And are therefore vague - For example: NPV will provide a numerical rate of return upon when the proposed investment into robotization will reach profitability.
Also - How long are you considering (3, 4 5 years - what?)

Methodology

	Source of Information	**Justification**
Primary Research	Interviews with: • GM • Financial manager (FM) • Production manager (PM)	• Collect qualitative data for FFA (driving, restraining forces) • Collect financial records from the FM and calculate the NPV together. • Collaborative work with PM to create the capacity utilization and productivity rate.
	Surveys to: • Sub division managers	• Collect further qualitative data for FFA from other sources to eliminate bias.

	• Directors of production	
	• Cooperation with Flabeg management	• Identifying the strengths, weaknesses, opportunities and threats to form a SWOT analysis.
Secondary Research	• Business management textbooks	• Guide through theoretical framework, tools as well as terminology in syllabus.
	• Online research	• States the advantages / disadvantages of industrial robots, with justification.

Anticipated Difficulties

Problems	Reasons	Solutions
Confidential financial data	Business may not want to reveal their financial data (for NPV).	Attempt to convince the GM with a letter of confidentiality.
Availability of key personnel	Not all personnel would be available the time I will want to interview them.	Contact all the personnel beforehand to create a schedule to fit everyone's time.
Bias	Responses to interview questions might be biased.	Use both closed and open questions to provide more responses and feedback

Table of Contents

1. Executive Summary

Flabeg is a global company that manufactures car mirrors in the automotive industry. The business has been facing problems with high labor costs, high scrap rates and low automation and obsolete technology, which has not helped with increasing profitability. In hopes to increase the profitability, the business has suggested investment into industrial robots to reduce labor costs, increase automation and provide quality and better performance, which created the research question: ***Should Flabeg invest into industrial robots to increase profitability?***

Research includes; Primary sources are interviews with GM, BU 11 Production Manager, Operation Director, Vice President of Finance, Industrial Engineering Manager and the collaborate work of the management. These secondary sources were used to investigate the investment into industrial robots; SWOT analysis, Force Field Analysis, Capacity Utilization Rate, Productivity Rate, Labor Productivity Rate and Net Present Value.

Main findings showed that investing into industrial robots would increase profitability (NPV) when cutting labor and replacing with robot, and would provide better efficiency and productivity than manual labor. Further, the weakness (SWOT) of low automation and obsolete technology would be improved. However, the business still struggles with capacity utilization due to damaged supplied material.

The final recommendation is to invest into industrial robots, decrease labor costs and increase profitability that way. Further recommendations include using outside sources of repair as well as potentially implementing this change in Flabeg globally.

However, the disadvantage of this investigation is the results obtained from the SWOT and FFA due to bias. As well as estimations used when calculating the NPV, thus reducing the validity of this investigation.

2. Introduction

2.1 Background

The business, Flabeg, was founded in 1889 in Nuremberg, Germany. It began with manufacturing both glass and mirrors and not just for automotive industries. The company progressed and expanded to further destinations, eight in total (Global). Flabeg Shanghai started up in 2004, and the core focus is on manufacturing automotive mirrors (see ***Figure 1***). The business has been progressively expanding for the last 10 years, and would like to sustain their market leader position.

As there have been many other businesses providing similar products in the market, Flabeg needs to focus on how to remain the market leader, as well as become a global leader. With a decent income stream of roughly 4,800,000RMB in the exterior mirror production line, the business is currently struggling with high unit costs due to labor costs, as well as high scrap rates. In hopes to increase the profitability, Flabeg has begun thinking about investing into industrial robots to decrease both labor costs as well as the scrap rate. However, further investigation and evaluation has to be conducted in order to find out whether or not investing into industrial robots is the correct decision for this business.

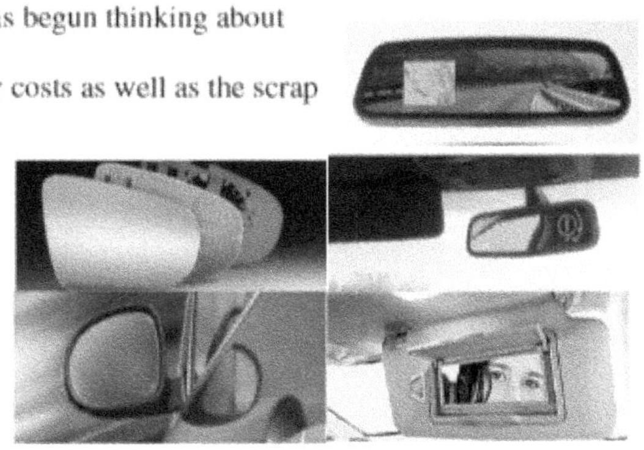

Figure 1 – Variety of Flabeg Car Mirrors

2.2 Research Question

Therefore, this investigation will use the following research question: ***Should Flabeg invest into industrial robots to increase profitability?***

3. Methodology

3.1 Primary research

1. Two interviews with the GM, Richard Gattringer. The preliminary will give understanding about the business and its struggles. This interview will also involve creating a SWOT analysis. The follow up interview will investigate his point of view and assessment on the change discussed. Two more interviews with the Vice President of Finance to discuss the NPV, and the Operations Director to calculate the capacity utilization rate, productivity rate and labor productivity rate.
2. Further, a questionnaire sent first, then collaboration with the Operation Director, the Industrial Engineering Manager and the BU11 Production Manager, to create a force field analysis.
3. Flabeg's financial reports to determine the net present value of their already existing investments.

3.2 Secondary research

1. China's market growth in the recent years (automotive mirrors)
2. Investopedia for terminological references
3. Business textbooks (tools used in investigation)

3.3 Tools and Techniques Chosen

1. *SWOT Analysis* is a decision-making tool that uses the acronym for Strengths, Weaknesses, Opportunities, Threats to asses both internal and external factors of a firm (HOANG 40).
2. *Force Field Analysis (FFA)* a decision-making tool that consists of driving forces for or driving forces against, that influence change within a firm (Stimpson and Smith 112).

3. *Net Present Value (NPV)* calculates the total discounted net cash flows taken away by the initial investment cost, which shows the firms profitability (Stimpson and Smith 320).
4. *Capacity Utilization Rate* measures a firms already existing level of output as a proportion output (Hoang 528).
5. *Productivity Rate* is a measure of how effectively the resources are being used during the production process (Hoang 530).

3.4 Validity and Reliability of Data

- The data from the capacity utilization rate are only estimations, hence the figures might be inaccurate.
- Personal bias, the people interviewed could have adjusted the data due to their opinions and biases. (Especially for FFA and SWOT)
- The NPV tool is a forecasting technique which could be proved inaccurate after some time, especially because the "discount rate" changes overtime.
- No customers were interviewed or surveyed; hence the data might be biased towards the firm.
- Not enough divisions of the firm were talked to (only managers and directors, no lower placed employee)

4. Main Results and Findings

4.1 Organizational Planning Tool

a. SWOT Analysis (***Appendix 1***)

Strengths:	**Weaknesses**:
- Experienced staff - Global brand with long history - Powerful sales team - Location of business - Quality - Multinational company	- Obsolete equipment - Low automation - Product price too high - Administration costs too high - Top management team unable to speak mandarin; communication with common employees is insufficient -
Opportunities:	**Threats**:
- Enter complimentary or substitute product markets that may use the same machine - Enlarge local market and aftermarket - New innovation / technology for improvement	- More competitors - New technology to replace rearview mirrors - Environmental costs / protection policy get stricter - Labor costs increase - Raw material costs increase

b. Force Field Analysis (***Appendix 2***)

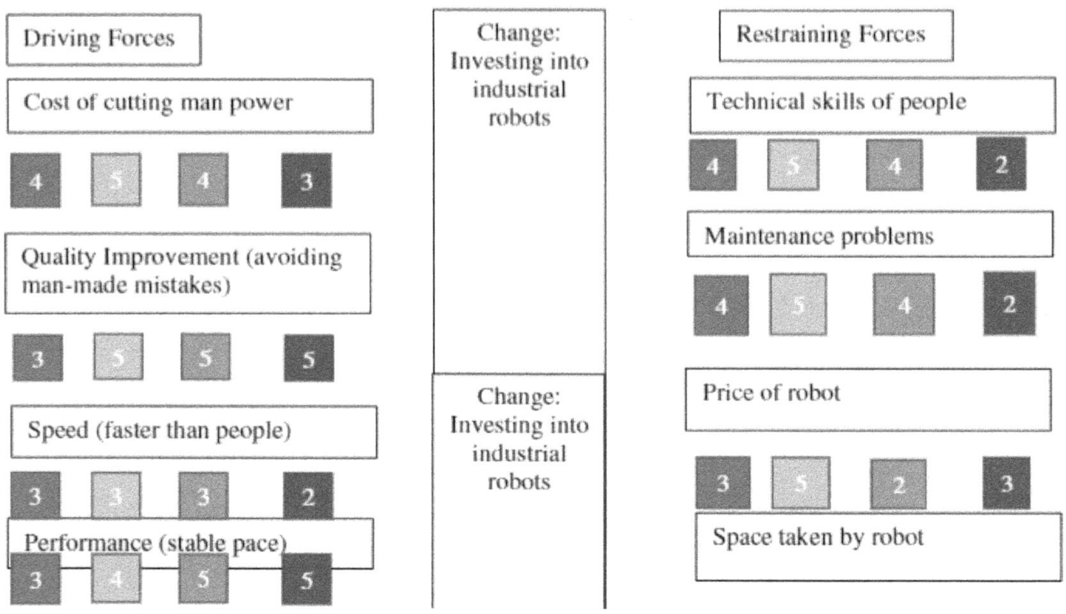

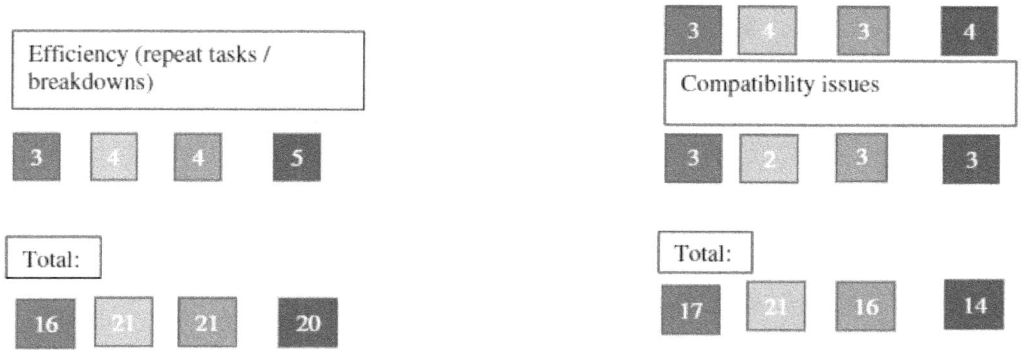

4.2 Investment Appraisal

a. NPV (*Appendix 3*)

Years	Cash Flow (RMB)	Discount factor (6%) – SYLLABUS Chart	Present Value (RMB)	Calculations
0	(424,779)	1	(424,779)	
1	192,000	0.9434	181,132.8	192,000x0.9434=181,132.8
2	384,000	0.8900	376,320	384,000x0.9800=376,320
3	384,000	0.8396	322,406.4	384,000x0.8396=322,406.4
4	384,000	0.7921	304,166.4	384,000x0.7921=304,166.4
5	384,000	0.7473	286,963.2	384,000x0.7473=286,963.2
6	379,000	0.7050	267,195	379,000x0.7050=267,195
7	379,000	0.6651	255,398.4	379,000x0.6651=252,072.9
8	379,000	0.6271	237,670.9	379,000x0.6271=237,670.9
9	379,000	0.5919	224,330.1	379,000x0.5919=224,330.1
10	379,000	0.5584	211,633.6	379,000x0.5584=211,633.6
Total Present Value			2,667,200	

$$Net\ Present\ Value = Present\ Value - Initial\ Investement$$

$$NPV = 2{,}667{,}200 - 424{,}779 = \mathbf{2,242,421RMB}$$

4.3 Production Planning

Current:

a. Capacity Utilization Rate (***Appendix 4***)

$$= \frac{actual\ output}{productive\ capacity} \times 100$$

$$= \frac{1{,}200{,}000}{1{,}500{,}000} \times 100$$

$$= 0.8 \times 100$$

$$= \mathbf{80\%}$$

b. Productivity Rate (***Appendix 6***)

$$= \frac{total\ output}{number\ of\ workers}$$

$$= \frac{1{,}200{,}000}{22 \times 12 \times 72}$$

$$= \frac{1{,}200{,}000}{19{,}008}$$

$= 63.1$ units per hour

With Machine:

a. Capacity Utilization Rate

b. Productivity Rate

5. Analysis & Discussion

5.1 Qualitative Data

SWOT Analysis

Based on the interview with the GM, Flabeg's biggest weaknesses come from having low automation, old equipment and high costs. Due to these internal weaknesses, the company faces external threats such as competitors having more automation and newer equipment which would outperform Flabeg. Further, based on the weaknesses the business is facing it could even face more threats such as customers replacing rearview mirrors with technology due to product pricing of rearview mirrors that Flabeg manufactures being too high. Despite all the negatives, the SWOT analysis also shows what the business is currently doing well, and could potentially achieve. Flabeg is a global brand that provides customers with quality products. Due to its good image, the business could potentially enter new markets, develop new products, enlarge the local market and aftermarket, and most importantly invest into equipment and technology.

That being said, looking at the opportunities from the SWOT analysis, through investment into equipment and technology, or in Flabeg's case, industrial robots, it could potentially decrease a number of weaknesses and threats the management has identified in the SWOT analysis (***Appendix 1***).

Force Field Analysis

For the force field analysis, the Operation Director, BU11 production manager as well as two other members of the production management worked together to identify driving forces for and restraining forces against investing into industrial robots. The FFA included an equal amount of driving and restraining forces, allowing for a more balanced analysis (***Appendix 2***). The result showed that when all members data combined the driving forces rank as more important than the restraining. This shows that the identified driving forces, such as quality improvement, performance and efficiency of the robot outweigh the restraining forces such as the technical skills of the employees, space taken up by the robot as well as maintenance problems. Through the interview, the reason why driving forces such as quality improvement and efficiency was ranked much higher than space and technical skills of people is that the quality of the product is directly linked with profitability. Quality is a key factor for customers, the higher the quality the more satisfaction. Further, the efficiency of the robot is directly linked to the labor costs, scrap rates and capacity utilization. A robot works much more efficiently than a human, it does not make man-made mistakes and does not need rest breaks or pauses. The less pauses there are the more mirrors can be made, which would increase the capacity utilization rate. The efficiency of the robot can also help with reducing scraps, due to more precision and accuracy. Lastly, the performance could help decrease the cost of manpower which decreases the labor costs.

5.2 Quantitative Data

Capacity Utilization Rate

The capacity utilization rate measures the actual output of the business in proportion to the full production capacity (Hoang 258). Through the use of an interview with the Operation Director, Roman ____, the actual output of the business is 1.2 million units per month, whereas the productive capacity is 1.5 million units per month. This shows that the capacity utilization rate is at 80% (***Appendix 4***). According to Roman, from an industrial point of view, 80% productivity is substantially low. However, as mentioned in the interview, that is due to the fact that Flabeg works with glass. Not only is it fragile, but Flabeg is also not attractive to suppliers. In order to manufacture car mirrors, not that much glass is needed and so Flabeg does not purchase as much glass as other customers of the suppliers. Being unattractive to the suppliers makes finding suppliers very difficult and because of that it allows the suppliers to deliver somewhat damaged glass which brings down the total output of the business.

Labor Productivity Rate

The labor productivity rate measures the efficiency of the workers in production and the total output per month (Hoang 530). The higher the productivity rate the more efficient the workers are. Based on data gathered from the interview with Roman _____, the labor productivity is 63.13 (***Appendix 6***). The business is not satisfied with this number because due to labor costs, this number is much lower than it should be. In the production line, many of the jobs the workers have could easily be replaced by robots, which would cut down the number of workers and shifts needed (decreased labor costs) as well as improve the efficiency and performance (decreased scrap rate). In the interview with the GM, the reason why the labor productivity isn't high enough is due to the labor costs increasing in Shanghai, as well as workers wanting increased income (Tang). Due to the increase in labor costs, the labor productivity rate is slowly decreasing, which disallows Flabeg from profitability. When implementing robots, they could easily replace the simple, tedious jobs the workers are doing, and function almost 24/7 without needing maintenance too often.

Net Present Value

NPV is an investment appraisal tool that calculates the present value of the business' future cash flow while including the discount factor to consider the money's change in value in the future (OXFORD 237). According to ____ the discount factor suitable for Flabeg is at 6%.

According to statistics, the discount factor has been slowly reducing within China, numbers ranging between 3.85% (recently) and 5.77% (2014 - 2016), hence the discount rate 6% is the most recognized rate in China ("China Loan Prime Rate). The NPV calculation is just a forecast of the future cash flows, however, the calculations ended up positive. The calculations included both investment cost, as well as the cost of maintenance yearly after the 5th year. Which according to my interview and force field analysis could be one of the biggest disadvantages the business could face with purchasing a robot.

As the robot is replacing working labor, the cash inflow in the NPV are the cut salaries of the workers. With that said, and maintenance costs of 5,000 RMB yearly for 5 out of the 10 years being put in, the business would gain profit by 2,242,421 RMB with an initial investment of 424,779 RM (***Appendix 3***). Instead of workers that need constant breaks, are inefficient, low in performance and demand higher salaries, which lead to high labor costs, the robot would work efficiently 24/7 which reduces the main weakness identified in the SWOT analysis, labor costs.

The restraining forces that were identified about this investment in the FFA are the workers that supervise this robot. The workers needed for supervision need to be more experienced with technology and understand the robot well. This could mean that the worker supervising the robot would have a higher salary, which cannot be identified within the NPV. Further, another concern about this would be that even though the robot would be working efficiently and with excellent performance the problems with increasing capacity utilization from just 80% is not just about increased efficiency, but also the problem with suppliers delivering damaged material.

6. Conclusion & Recommendations

6.1 Conclusion

According to the qualitative findings, the SWOT analysis identified the biggest weakness being low automation and obsolete technology. Another weakness identified within an interview with the GM suggests that the business is lacking profitability due to high labor costs and scrap rates. This all suggests for a new approach towards increasing profitability, hence, investment in to industrial robots. The FFA showed the judgement of four professionals in this field, using this organizational planning tool, the results showed that the driving forces towards implementing this change outweigh the restraining forces.

Furthermore, quantitative data suggests that the capacity utilization rate of 80% must be improved, and the simplest way to this approach would be through the efficient work of robots. Although the low-capacity utilization rate is also affected by the damaged materials supplied, one way of improving it would be through increased performance and efficiency that the robot could implement. The labor productivity rate showed us that the productivity of the workers is lacking. Due to the high labor costs Flabeg is facing, the productivity of the workers is very important. However, because the productivity isn't where it should be, robots replacing labor would cost Flabeg less money, and increase profitability, this can be seen through the NPV. The NPV for the future robot suggests an increase in profitability by 2,242,421 RMB. ***Therefore, in conclusion, Flabeg should invest into robots to increase its profitability***

6.2 Reflection

The FFA Analysis was done with four individuals, which I believe collects a more reliable set of data. However, this method of data collecting is subjective and according to personal (but also professional) bias, which does not make it 100% reliable.

The SWOT analysis was done by the Flabeg management, but maybe not every opinion was heard, and more points could have been added to it.

The NPV is just a prediction of how the investment would influence profitability. Though maintenance was included in the calculation, that is just an estimation on how much the costs would be, based on the damage of the robot it could cost more/less. However, due to it being an estimation, all of the data inputted in the calculation is just a conjecture.

6.3 Final Recommendation

1. Make sure to train Flabeg employees to assist the robot and understand the processes it undergoes, through the use of an experienced mechanic.
2. Do not hire employees that will know how to fix the robot, this will increase labor costs as they are professionals, and the alternative option of using an outside source for repair is cheaper in the long run.
3. Continue using investment appraisal tools to analyze the success of the investment.

6.4 Further Study

- Implementing investment into industrial robots in more Flabeg firms, after seeing the results with investment in Flabeg Shanghai.

BIBLIOGRAPHY + APPENDICES OMITTED

5. EXAMPLE FIVE (25/25)

Name: 'Should XYZ discontinue psychiatric Telehealth services for all patients to better manage their face-to-face appointments?

Author: Anonymous

Session: November 2022

Level: HL

Research question:

Should ███ discontinue psychiatric Telehealth services for all patients to better manage their face-to-face appointments?

Rationale:

███ is a private limited company located in Toowong, Brisbane, providing face-to-face and telehealth (online) psychiatric appointments. Through these services, ███ has been catering to the growing demand for psychiatric care within Australia. Resultingly, ███ is struggling to manage its excessive waiting list and workload, instigating its consideration of removing Telehealth services from its product portfolio to improve care quality. Regardless, this may limit the growth potential of the firm.

Theoretical framework:

<u>Areas of the syllabus to be covered:</u>

1.3 SWOT analysis: determining the internal and external factors currently affecting ███, and the feasibility of discontinuing telehealth

1.7 Lewin's Force Field analysis: evaluating the restraining and driving forces regarding ███'s discontinuation of Telehealth

3.5 Profitability ratio analysis: analysing ███'s financial position, while determining the implications which discontinuing telehealth will have on this

1.7 Fishbone diagram: visually representing the causes of the time management problems affecting ███, to determine the impact of ending Telehealth services on these issues

Data collection (sources of information and rationale link):

Table 1: data collection methods

Primary or secondary:	**Type of data collection:**	**Source**	**Purpose**
Primary	Interview	Owner of ███	Evaluating the current nature of the service provided, and area for growth

	Questionnaire	Psychiatrists in the ████████ ███ who currently provide telehealth service	Evaluating the experiences of psychiatrists in a similar situation to ████, regarding telehealth
	Observation	████████ ███	Quantifying and comparing Telehealth and face-to-face appointments which run overtime
Secondary	Weekly schedule	Owner of ████	Quantifying the various platforms used to deliver ████'s appointments daily
	Financial data collection	Profit & loss account	Completing the profitability analysis for this year and the forecasted next 2 years (assuming telehealth is discontinued), by identify areas of downfall or success
	Additional statistics	Other websites	Identifying external factors affecting ████'s operations

Planning:

Table 2: Planning

Anticipated difficulties	Anticipated solutions
Biased interview and questionnaire responses, affecting the validity of conclusions drawn	Provide the owner and respondents with letters of confidentiality, ensuring their confidence in communicating truthful information
Limited information provided through questionnaire and interview responses	Predominantly ask open-ended but specific questions, maximising quality, relevant responses
Biased data from observations as they are only conducted during a specific period	Collate data over a wide period of 5 weeks while visiting the clinic often, improving accuracy and reliability
Patient confidentiality requirements limiting patient information collated	Collect a range of information regarding the impact of services on patients through the questionnaire to other psychiatrists and interview with ████'s owner

Gantt Chart:

Table 1: Gantt chart

Action	Date										Modifications
	May	June	July	Aug	Sep	Oct	Nov	Dec	Jan	Feb	
Develop interview questions											Added more questions later
Interview owner											-
Develop questionnaire questions											-
Distribute questionnaires to respondents											-
Collate secondary data											-
Complete profitability analysis											-
Complete SWOT analysis											-
Complete Lewin's forcefield diagram											Added more restraining forces
Complete fishbone diagram											Changed main issue identified
Write full report											-
Draft IA due											-
Edit IA based on draft feedback											Continued editing in January
Format document											-
Discuss results of the investigation with ████											-
Final IA due											-

Table of Contents

Executive summary:

The owner of █████ has expressed difficulty with managing her schedule and rising demand, increasing appointment waiting times. Moreover, with Medicare proposing to limit telehealth rebate provisions by December 2022, alongside the concern that both telehealth and face-to-face appointments could not be provided without compromising quality, the owner proposed the discontinuation of telehealth to combat this issue.

Following this, primary research was conducted through an interview with █████'s owner, observations of overtime appointments, and questionnaires sent to other psychiatrists providing telehealth and face-to-face care within the ████████████. This information was utilized in the SWOT analysis, Lewin's forcefield analysis and Fishbone diagram, to qualitatively analyse the state of the business, and the implications of discontinuing telehealth on this. Secondary data was collated through █████'s 2021 profit and loss account, alongside forecasted accounts for 2022 and 2023 after discontinuing telehealth, to produce a profitability analysis, gauging the impact of discontinuing telehealth on █████'s financial position.

The conclusion suggests that █████'s optimal profitability ratios alongside opportunities to improve local market penetration would strengthen profitability and care quality. Hence, the discontinuation of telehealth is recommended. Regardless, it is recommended to conduct further market research, ensuring the solidarity of the proposed recommendations.

Word count: 199

Introduction

██████ PTY LTD. is a private limited company founded on the 1st of October 2018 by ██████, its only shareholder and director, with her secretary as her only employee. ██████ offers psychiatric services to a wide demographic of outpatients of 16-65 years of age, facing a range of mental illnesses. Its mission statement is to 'provide the best quality care for patients in need.'[1]

██████ offers face-to-face or online appointments (called telehealth), through audio or video conferences, all from a room which she rents in the ██████, Brisbane. Currently, while all appointments are priced at $290 per half hour, Medicare funds $160 of this through rebates.[2] Although, Medicare has proposed to stop providing telehealth rebates to patients within a 15km radius of the clinic by December of 2022.[3] Nevertheless, with ██████'s customer base steadily increasing with a rising demand for mental health support in Queensland,[4] ██████ has struggled with an excessive waiting list and workload.[5] This leads to the question, **Should ██████ discontinue psychiatric Telehealth services for all patients to better manage their face to face appointments?**

Methodology

This investigation combines three primary and two secondary sources of data to substantiate SWOT, Forcefield, profitability and Fishbone analyses, developing a thorough conclusion. The interview with the owner identified ██████'s current situation and objectives. The questionnaire with other telehealth-providing psychiatrists in The ██████ evaluated the performance of Telehealth and in-clinic services. The observation at ██████'s consulting room quantified ██████'s telehealth and face-to-face appointments which ran overtime.

Similarly, the secondary data obtained through ██████'s weekly schedule quantified the Telehealth appointments provided through video and audio conferences. The current profit and loss (P/L) account had been audited by Medicare, ensuring its reliability and the subsequent accuracy of the forecasted P/L accounts used in the profitability analysis. The data collected through the Australian Government's Medicare Benefits Schedule (MBS) fact sheet was from the most recent publication (as of December 2021), ensuring relevance.

---

[1] Appendix 1
[2] Appendix 1
[3] (MBS online, 2021)
[4] (University of Queensland, 2021)

Main results and findings

The interview with the owner revealed that the business's demand has increased over time correlating with an increase in speciality (through upskilling) and recognition.[6] █████ is currently focusing on its objective to reduce waiting lists, considering past patient complaints regarding waiting times, to reduce the "adverse outcomes of delayed care."[7] Overall, the company prioritises the quality of care provided over profitability.[8]

66.66% of questionnaire respondents introduced telehealth services into their product portfolio within the last 2 years.[9] Key statistics include:

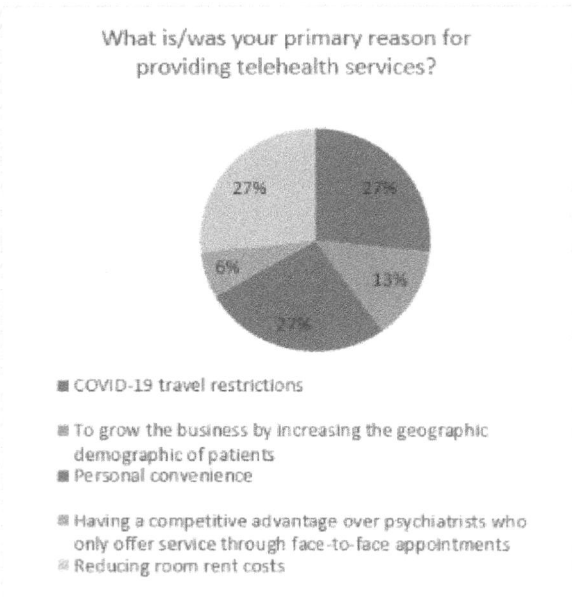

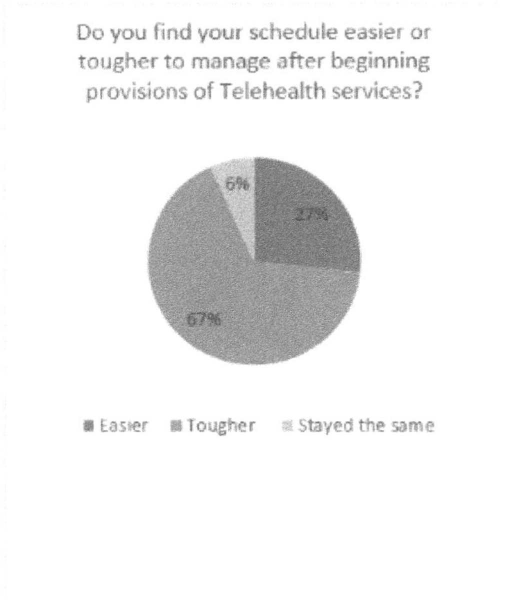

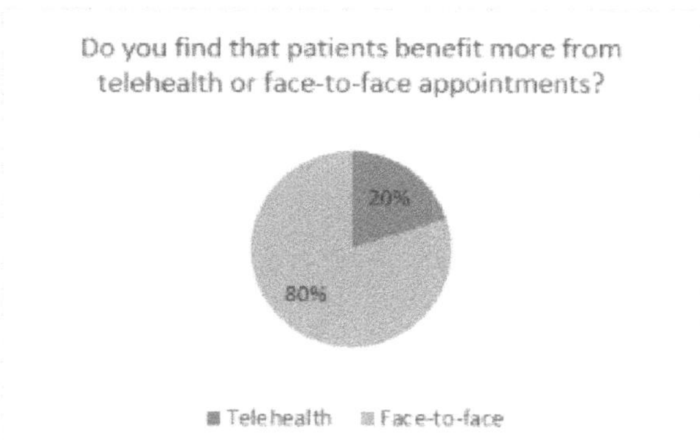

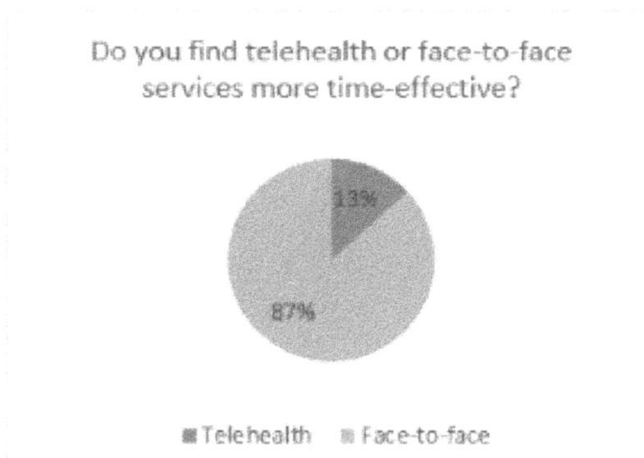

Figure 1: questionnaire responses

The observation at ██████'s consulting room determined that 59.13% of appointments went overtime.[10] These overtime appointments consisted of:

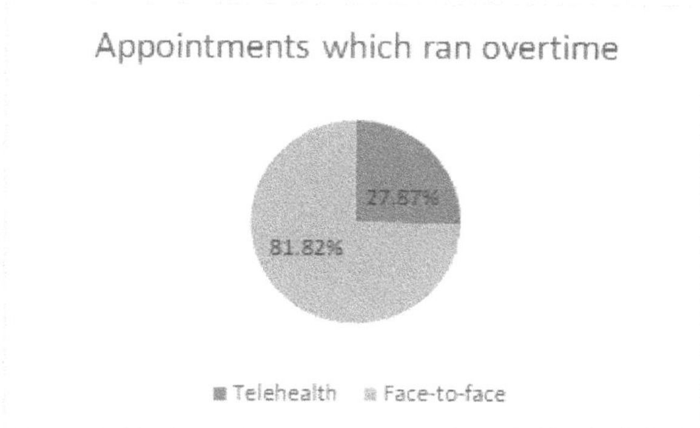

Figure 2: Observation of overtime appointments

On average, ██████ provided approximately 4 face-to-face and 4 telehealth appointments daily.[11]

Analysis and Evaluation

SWOT analysis:

The SWOT analysis investigated the current situation of ██████, to assist with assessing the feasibility of removing telehealth from ██████'s product portfolio.

Table 1: SWOT analysis

Internal factors	
Strengths	***Weaknesses***
• Reputable clinic • Variety of appointment methods for patients • Translating services maximise the culture demographic of patients[12] • Rebates provided by Medicare • As a registered company, unconditionally paying only 30% of profits as tax[13] • Only financed through retained profits, avoiding interest charges[14]	• Full schedule and waiting list[15] • Reduced efficiency of telehealth • No additional employees assisting with workload[16] • No remuneration for completing patient reports • Responsibility to bulk-bill some patients[17] • Unlimited liability
External factors	
Opportunities	***Threats***
• Demand for mental health service after COVID-19 pandemic[18] • Advertising benefits through the clinic • Expected national fall in unemployment reducing bulk-billings[19]	• Growing workload • Patient disagreement with psychiatric diagnoses[20] • Increased privacy risk when online for telehealth • Competition from 28 other psychiatrists in the clinic • Poorer broadband services for rural patients[21] • Medicare proposing to limit provisions of telehealth rebates • Highly bureaucratic Medicare policies[22]

---

[12] Appendix 1
[13] (Business – Australian Government, 2021)
[14] Appendix 1
[15] Appendix 1
[16] Appendix 1
[17] (RANZCP, 2021)

The ████████████████ has been accredited by the Royal Australian and New Zealand college of Psychiatrists,[23] contributing to ██████'s thriving reputation, improving patient trust, local word-of-mouth advertising and referrals.

Nevertheless, alongside its poor time management, ██████ has experienced patient disagreements with ████████'s psychiatric analyses,[24] possibly due to limited patient insight into their situation. This may be caused by the poorer patient-psychiatric interaction through telehealth services than face-to-face services (particularly the 32% of appointments delivered through audio call), [25] as claimed by 93.33% of questionnaire respondents.[26]

Although, telehealth services facilitate organizational growth through a wide customer base, which █ ██████ could cater to considering her upskilling courses and specialisation. Moreover, ██████ benefits from the person culture within the clinic, with support from other psychiatrists and promotion through the clinic's website.[27] Additionally, an expected fall in Australia's unemployment rate by 4.5% by December 2022 and again in December 2023[28] could reduce bulk billed patients (as patients are bulk-billed when they are financially struggling),[29] increasing profitability.

However, while Medicare proposed that only patients residing outside of the metropolitan (15km away from the clinic) can access rebated telehealth, the poor internet access amongst Australian rural communities[30] could reduce time efficiency of telehealth, with 87% of questionnaire respondents finding telehealth less time efficient than face-to-face appointments.[31]

Lewin's Force field analysis:

The force field diagram evaluated the driving and restraining forces concerning ██████'s discontinuation of telehealth services. Each force is ranked out of 5 regarding importance, as determined in consultation with ██████'s owner:

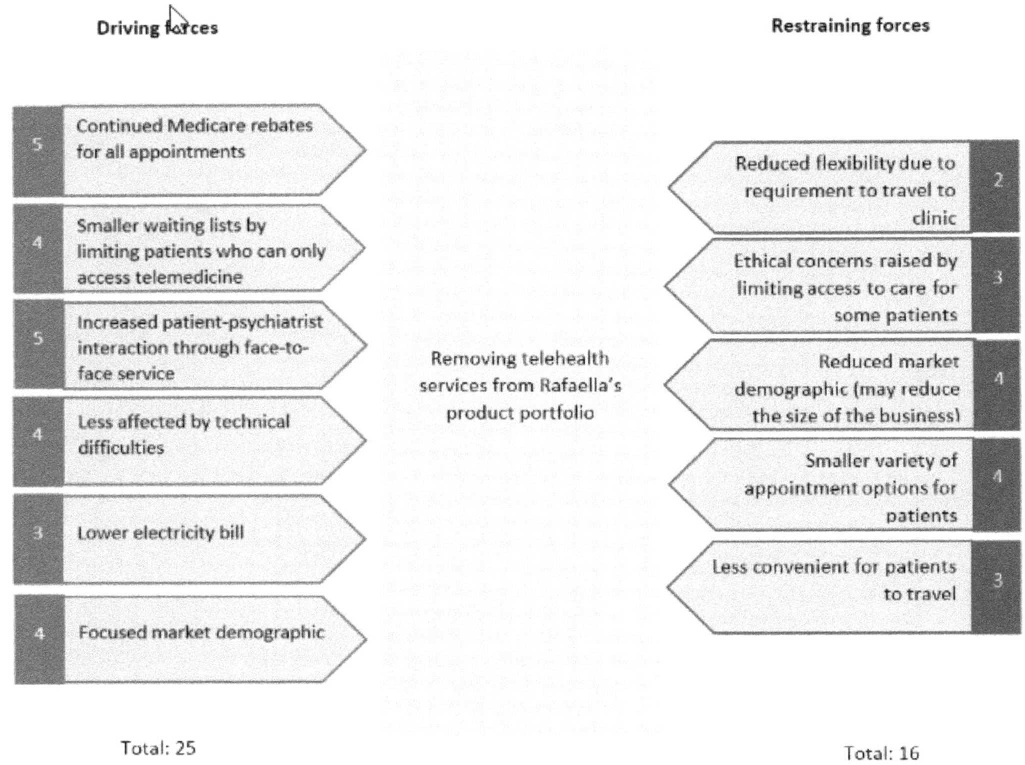

Figure 3: Forcefield diagram

With Medicare planning on limiting access to telehealth rebates, patients within 15 km of ██████ would have to pay $160 more per half hour for telehealth appointments.[32] While this surge in prices should be justified through quality care, 80% of questionnaire respondents found that patients benefitted more through face-to-face services,[33] suggesting the difficulty of providing better quality telehealth services. Alternatively, only providing face-to-face services ensures continued rebates for all appointments, maintaining affordability and customer satisfaction; giving this force a high score of 5/5.

Approximately 50% of daily appointments are delivered through telehealth.[34] Hence, removing these would decrease █████'s customer base and subsequently its waiting list (with 66.66% of survey respondents finding their schedule more manageable before introducing telehealth appointments).[35] Resultingly, █████ could achieve its objective of reducing waiting times to prevent the adverse outcomes of delayed care.[36] Thus, this force demonstrated a high score of 4/5.

Discontinuing telehealth could reduce █████'s customer base to individuals within the metropolitan, facilitating market penetration through targeted upskilling. Furthermore, with approximately 90% of █████'s patients aged 25-34,[37] this age group occupies the highest percentage (16.2%) of Australians living in capital cities, including Brisbane.[38] Hence, █████'s current patient age demographic remains mostly supported by discontinuing Telehealth, minimalizing the risk of doing so. This force therefore had a high score of 4/5.

Nevertheless, discontinuing telehealth would limit the variety of appointment options provided, enforcing a requirement to travel to the clinic while reducing patient autonomy and satisfaction, particularly without a new marketing mix. This therefore produced a high ranking of 4/5.

While ethical concerns may arise regarding limiting care to some patients, █████'s limited capacity indicates the impracticality of the company providing care to all potential patients without overscheduling and compromising quality care. Therefore, this force demonstrated a mediocre score of 3/5.

The driving forces outweighed the restraining forces by 9 points, with quantitative and qualitative factors evidently indicating that █████ should remove telehealth services from its product portfolio.

Profitability analysis (AUD$)[39]:

During 2021:

Gross profit margin:

$$\frac{Gross\ profit}{Total\ revenue} \times 100\% = \frac{450{,}900}{450{,}900} \times 100\% = 100\%$$

Net profit margin:

$$\frac{Net\ profit}{Total\ revenue} \times 100\% = \frac{219{,}030}{450{,}900} \times 100\% = 48.58\%$$

Forecasted for 2022:

Gross profit margin:

$$\frac{Gross\ profit}{Total\ revenue} \times 100\% = \frac{403{,}000}{403{,}000} \times 100\% = 100\%$$

Net profit margin:

$$\frac{Net\ profit}{Total\ revenue} \times 100\% = \frac{185{,}500}{403{,}000} \times 100\% = 46.03\%$$

Forecasted for 2023:

Gross profit margin:

$$\frac{Gross\ profit}{Total\ revenue} \times 100\% = \frac{465{,}000}{465{,}000} \times 100\% = 100\%$$

Net profit margin:

$$\frac{Net\ profit}{Total\ revenue} \times 100\% = \frac{228{,}900}{465{,}000} \times 100\% = 49.23\%$$

The forecasted P/L account developed in consultation with ██████'s owner predicted a fall in revenue in the first year after discontinuing telehealth (2022), due to a reduced customer base. Regardless, while the gross profit margin is consistently 100% since expenditures only involve operating expenses, the net profit margin (NPM) is more relevant to the investigation.

██████'s currently high NPM of 48.58% indicates that retained profits are sufficient to facilitate market research and targeted upskilling, encouraging word-of-mouth advertising through quality care.

With the subsequent expected overall increase in the NPM by 0.65% in the second year, additional retained profits could be reinvested into upskilling, ██████'s consultant room, and psychiatric resources (such as software to help manage appointments); capitalising on quality care.

Fish bone diagram:

The fishbone diagram evaluated the root causes and effects of a problem faced by ██████. This will assist in determining whether removing telehealth would improve, or be jeopardised by these concerns.

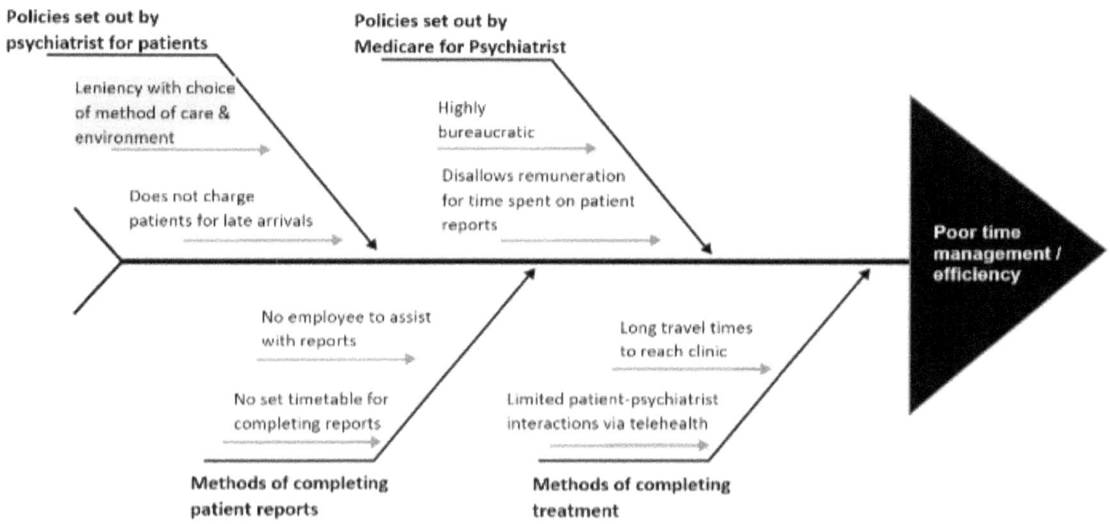

Figure 4: Fishbone diagram

The primary issue causing poor time management (as highlighted in blue) is that ██████ allows patients to choose their appointment method (telehealth or face-to-face) and their environment for telehealth appointments, increasing distractions during telehealth appointments[40]. This could reduce patient-psychiatrist interactions, hindering the efficiency and quality of care. Moreover, ██████'s leniency with late arrivals could instigate the 59.19% of appointments which run overtime,[41] potentially disturbing the appointment schedule, while reducing ██████'s revenue (as prices are determined by the duration of appointments)[42] unless the psychiatrist works overtime. The resultant poor coordination could prevent ██████ from fulfilling its objective of reducing waiting periods.

This issue is exacerbated by the highly bureaucratic Medicare pricing policies, including ██████ only being permitted to charge patients for appointments of any duration under the actual duration of the provided appointment.[43] The overall lack of remuneration may reduce motivation, efficiency and quality of reports and services. While Medicare policies are uncontrollable, removing telehealth services could increase ██████'s control over its patients' environment (in the consultant room) to decrease distractions; increasing the efficiency and quality of care. Subsequently, this could motivate patients to arrive promptly for quality appointments.

Conclusion

All four tools demonstrated that ██████ should discontinue telehealth services. The SWOT analysis indicated that ██████ has sufficient strengths and opportunities to sustain face-to-face services, while several underlined weaknesses and threats could be avoided by discontinuing telehealth. In the Lewin's Forcefield analysis, the vast list of quantitative and qualitative driving forces significantly outweighed the restraining forces regarding discontinuing telehealth. Correspondingly, the profitability analysis indicated that ██████ was financially supported to undertake this change. While the fishbone diagram presented no major concerns which opposed the discontinuation of telehealth, this change could diminish some presented problems. Nevertheless, ██████'s vulnerability to external threats such as local competitors may reduce its demand and profitability.

Recommendations

1. ██████ should focus on eliminating key problems identified in the fishbone analysis by strategically scheduling its time, particularly for completing reports. Moreover, the business should send patients reminders before appointments to encourage prompt arrivals, improving time efficiency.

2. ██████ should also conduct local market research to facilitate effective market penetration in the regional market. With this, ██████ should utilise its increasing retained profits for targeted upskilling courses for this market demographic, improving the quality of care.

3. Additionally, to maintain local demand regardless of competitors, ██████ should conduct research through "Porter's five forces" to develop an understanding of opportunities and threats from competitors.

Limitations

While patients could not be used as sources of data due to patient confidentiality policies, the psychiatrists surveyed to provide information of patient experiences may have provided inaccurate, biased responses. Additionally, assumptions had to be made regarding ██████ having sufficient local patients to maintain purely face-to-face services, based on the clinic being located near the city.

BIBLIOGRAPHY + APPENDICES OMITTED

6. EXAMPLE SIX (24/25)

Name: 'Should North Al-Hail LLC expand its business to hotel and hospital industries to increase their profits?

Author: Anonymous

Session: May 2022

Level: HL

Research Proposal

Research question:

Should North Al-Hail LLC expand its business to hotel and hospital industries to increase their profits?

Rationale For Study:

North Al-Hail LLC is currently manufacturing industrial uniforms specially related to oil field[1], e.g.: coveralls of cotton, fireproof coveralls, and chemical proof coveralls. The business started in 2005[2] and have been steady with their production and sales up until 2014 where oil prices have reduced drastically[3], which affected NAH for the first time[4]. Additionally, the recent pandemic has also increased the negative impacts as it challenged their profits[5].

In order for NAH to solve this dilemma the owner of NAH has seen that the hotel industry in Oman is booming due to the increase in Tourism in Oman. As well as, the hospital industry because of the covid-19 pandemic[6]. Both industries require uniform wear, hence, the owner is considering to expand its business towards hotel and hospital industries to gain back their profits[7].

Proposed Methodology:

Areas of the Syllabus to be covered:
1.7 Organization planning tools: Force Field analysis
3.5 Profitability and liquidity ratio analysis: GPM, GR, ROCE,NPM, to evaluate the current financial position of the firm, whether it is capable of diversifying its business.
3.8: Investment appraisal: payback period.
4.2 Marketing planning: Exploring if NAH LCC has the abilities to move into the expansion given the capabilities of their tailors and the infrastructure of the company.

Possible Sources of Information:

- Owner and manager of the business
- Business employees
- Hotel experts
- Ministry of health
- Hotels in Oman

---

[1] Appendix 1- First interview with NAH owner.
[2] Appendix 1- First interview with NAH owner.
[3] https://www.atlanticcouncil.org/blogs/menasource/after-the-coronavirus-and-low-oil-prices-omans-future-is-more-global/
[4] Appendix 1- First interview with NAH owner.
[5] Appendix 1- First interview with NAH owner.
[6] Appendix 1- First interview with NAH owner.
[7] Appendix 1- First interview with NAH owner.

Organizations and Individuals to be approached:

- Adnan Al-Qadri and Hakim Al-Zadjali owners and managers of NAH.
- Adnan Al-Qadri financial director
- Mr Karim William, hotel expert and manager of local five-star hotel in Oman
- Employees of NAH
- Potential B2B customers

Methods used to collect and analyse data:

Primary research:

- Interview with owner, manager and financial director Adnan Al-Qadri to discuss the current difficulties and the consideration for change to overcome the dilemma.
- Approach an hotel expert Mr.Karim William to understand the future growth of tourism from the perspective of hotel industries
- Questionnaire for employees of North Al-Hail to check their technical expertise on whether they can produce a new product different from the product that is currently being produced. Additionally, whether recruitment of new employees will require training.
- Questionnaire for hotel industries around Oman, to gather competitors and potential future customers for NAH.

Secondary research:

- Research economic data on the future growth of Oman's economy
- Balance sheet and profit and loss account to calculate NPM, CR, and GR.
- Search online sewing machinery for cheaper prices
- Attempt to obtain financial record to calculate investment appraisal

Anticipated Difficulties:

Anticipated Difficulties	Anticipated solutions
Unable to access another interview with owner of NAH	In the first interview try to access as much information by asking more straightforward and logical questions. Additionally, gain trust with the owner of NAH
Financial and marketing secrets	logical approximation of the financial information provided based on primary and secondary research.
Not being able to access interview from hotel departments	Due to COVID managers from hotels might not agree, give them the option to interview them online.
Bias information from Questionnaire	Include Fewer more open questions to maximize quality qualitative responses.

Action Plan:

Action	Date	Modification
Start planning IA	9-6-2021	
Draft questions for interview with owner of NAH	10-6-2021	
Interview NAH owner and collect all secondary date	22-6-2021	
Draft the rest of primary data.	25-6-20212	
Collect all primary Date	20-7-2021	
Analyze primary and secondary date	22-7-2021	
Write up investigation	25-7-2021	
First Draft due	11- 11-2021	
Make edits based on feedback	13-12-2021	
Discuss results with NAH firm	4-2-2022	
Final IA Due	6-2-2022	

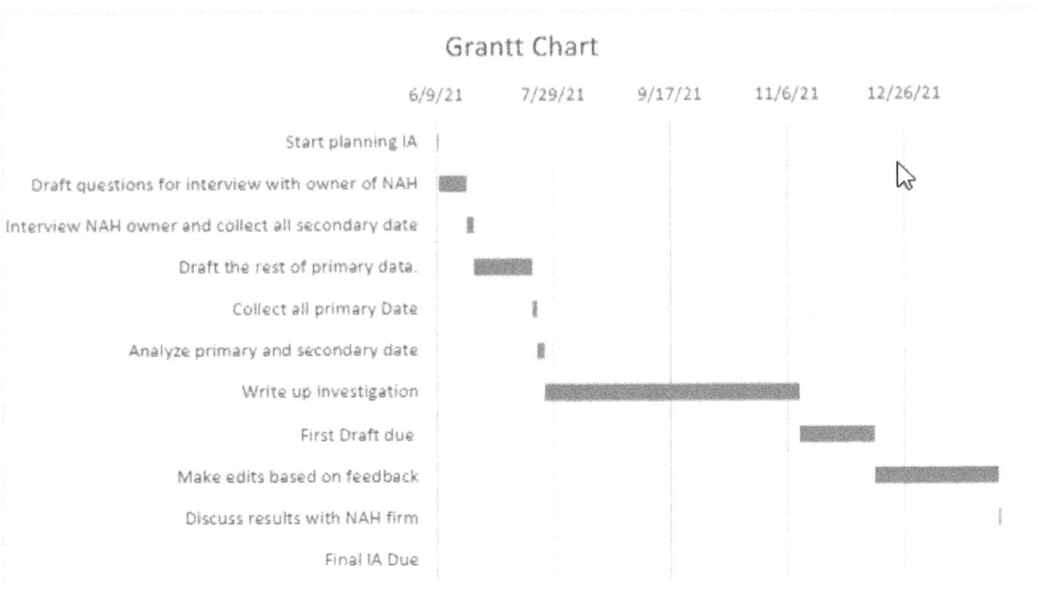

Table of Contents

Executive Summary:

North Al-Hail LLC is a garment manufacturer and exporter that cater the local need in industrial work force. Currently, due to the dip in oil prices internationally, which dragged the local petroleum companies to cost-cutting and because of the COVID-19 pandemic. Customers and companies have been requesting a reduction in NAH's products[8]. Hence, reducing their profits. In order for NAH to gain back their profits, it aims to enter to hotel and hospital industries because they have been significantly growing in Oman. Therefore, this report aims to answer the research question:

Should North Al-Hail LLC expand its business to hotel and hospital industries to increase their profits?

Primary research was conducted through interviews with internal stakeholders, an employee and hotel industries questionnaire. The information collected was presented using:
Force field analysis- driving forces outweighed restraining forces. Ratio analysis- figures suggest NAH is capable of expansion. Investment Appraisal Payback period of 10.9 months indicating low risk of investment.

Secondary research contained a balance sheet and profit & loss account as well as research on Oman's economy, potential competitors, and growth of the tourism sector.

Recommend NAH to go with the expansion, starting, with hotel industries first, then based of the success expand to hospital industries.

Word count: 200

---

[8] Appendix 8- Email send to North Al-Hail requesting reduction of prices.

1: Introduction:

North Al-Hail (NAH) is a limited liability company, with a partnership founded by Adnan Al-Qadri and Hakim Al-Zadjali on November the 14th 2004[9]. It specializes in catering the local need of coveralls for industrial work force.[10]

When the business started it was very successful, however, with the recent dip in oil prices and the Covid-19 pandemic many companies are requesting NAH to reduce their product prices due to the economic downturns[11]. Due to this the owner of NAH have been looking into different industries to manufacture uniforms for them in order to solve this dilemma of decreasing profits[12]. Currently, the hotel industry in Oman is booming due to the increase in the tourism sector, as well as, the hospital industry because of the ongoing Covid-19 pandemic. This has cause NAH to think about expanding their business into Hotel and Hospital industries to overcome this dilemma. It believes that making this decision a top priority for the business will not only regain their profits but also significantly increase them[13].

Therefore, my report tries to answer the research question:
Should *North Al-Hail LLC* expand its business to hotel and hospital industries to increase their profits?

2: Methodology Employed:

Primary research:

- **Interviews with owner of NAH[14]:** a detailed outline of the objectives of the business and their current performances and obtain financial information about expansion. Additionally, discussion of the financial and non-financial analysis gathered with the owner of NAH.
- **Interview with a hotel expert[15]:** Helped further conclude whether North Al Hail should expand to hotel industries and potential competitors.
- **Questionnaire with potential B2B customers from hotel industries in Oman[16]:** Pin point whether local hotels are interested in a local hotel uniform manufacture, and their point of view regarding the tourism in Oman and find potential competitors.
- **Questionnaire for NAH employees[17]:** analyze whether the employees of North Al-Hail are comfortable with the idea of expansion and whether they have the ability to produce soft wear clothing or train the possible new employees.

9 Appendix 1-First interview with owner of North Al-Hail
10 Appendix 1-First interview with owner of North Al-Hail
11 Appendix 8- Email send to North Al-Hail requesting reduction of prices.
12 Appendix 1-First interview with owner of North Al-Hail
13 Appendix 1-First interview with owner of North Al-Hail
14 Appendix 1-First interview with owner of North Al-Hail & Appendix 2- Second interview with NAH owner about the financial and non-financial analysis
15 Appendix 3 - Interview with a manager from the marketing department of hotels Mr. Karim William
16 Appendix 5- Questionnaire for Hotel Industries.
17 Appendix 4- Questionnaire for North Al-Hail employees

Note: All primary research techniques where piloted and checked by close relatives and friends that own businesses. Additionally, all information gathered helped me construct my Force Field Analysis, Ratio analysis, investment appraisal and conclude potential competitors that may interfere with the expansion.

Secondary research:

- Exact financial data were not shared due to confidential reasons, however, estimates where provided by financial director for the profit and loss account[18] and balance sheet[19] and cash flow for investment appraisal[20].
- Economic data on the future growth of Oman's economy.

Note: Financial data for this investigation is not official data but rather estimates. The variation of estimated figures reduces validity. Although, all financial accounts produced are both internally and externally reviewed which increase reliability and validity of conclusions.

3: Main Results and Findings:

The owner's aim to expand to hotel and hospital industries lies within his desire to improve his company's sales and increases the profit. While his first plan was to start with hotel industries due to governments motivations to improve tourism, he thought that *"hotel industries are technically the same, as far as tailoring, as hospital industries. So, I might as well kill two birds in one stone."*[21]

3.1: Competition in the market:

The potential competitors of North Al-Hail in supplying hotel and hospital uniforms is the, 'The green leaf for trading', 'Al-Safa uniforms' and 'white star tailors' that is based in Muscat. The barriers of these markets are potentially low as the uniform manufacturer market is known to be an easy market to get in to. However, competition is high as these businesses are known to be the top uniform manufactures in Oman due to its high customer services and good quality of products. 'White Star tailors' currently has customers from the hotel industries like the Kempinski hotel[22]. In order for NAH to survive and succeed in this market they would need a Unique selling point.

3.2: Hotel and hospital Industries:

As Oman is diversifying its economy, hotels industries are expected to grow by 28.3%[23] and hospital industries by 9.1%[24] in 2022. NAH will have an advantage to advertise their uniform

[18] Appendix 7- Profit and loss account
[19] Appendix 6- Balance Sheet
[20] Appendix 2- Second interview with NAH owner about the financial and non-financial analysis
[21] Appendix 1- First interview with owner of North Al-Hail
[22] Appendix 3 - Interview with a manager from the marketing department of hotels Mr. Karim William
[23] https://www.statista.com/statistics/1230257/oman-forecasted-revpar-muscat-change/#:~:text=Forecasted%20y%2Do%2Dy%20change%20of%20RevPAR,COVID%2D19%20Oman%202019%2D2024&text=The%20year%2Don%2Dyear%20change,be%2014.9%20percent%20in%202024.
[24] https://www.omanobserver.om/article/59652/Business/omans-healthcare-spend-to-reach-49bn-in-2022

company to the upcoming hotels and hospitals as is a growing market, therefore, gaining sales in this expansion and potentially increasing their profits.

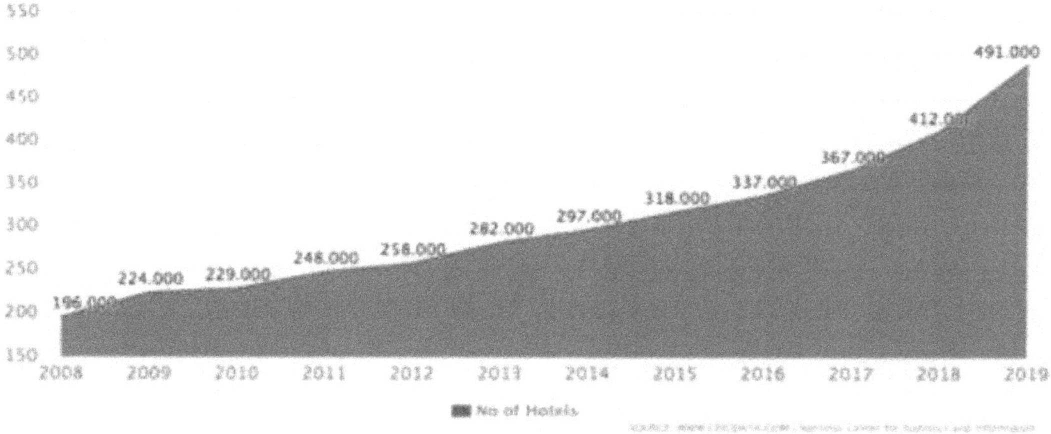

Figure 1.1: Number of hotels in Oman from the year of 2008 to 2019[25]
Plus 96 hotels in Oman are expected to start construction by the end of 2021[26]

3.3: Primary data collected:

1- The first interview with the Owner of NAH revealed that:

- His business is in good shape[27], as shown in the table 1.

  Table one[28]:

	2019	2020	Change (%)
Revenue	226,726	209,094	(7.78)
Gross Profit	48,656	44,128	(9.31)
Net Profit	8,716	2,434	(72.1)

- Some companies are requesting NAH to reduce their product prices due to the economic downturns[29], which indicates that this is a reason to move away from oil sectors and expand into hotel industries.
- Pandemic has caused the market to delay their payments[30], as shown in the balance sheet[31] the debtor days has changed from 2019 to 2020 by 5.39%.

[25] https://www.ceicdata.com/en/oman/hotel-statistics/no-of-hotels

[26] https://timesofoman.com/article/2841540/Oman/Tourism/96-hotels-are-expected-to-open-by-2021)

[27] Appendix 1- First interview with owner of North Al-Hail

[28] Appendix 7- Profit and loss account

[29] Appendix 1- First interview with owner of North Al-Hail & Appendix 8- Email send to North Al-Hail requesting reduction of prices.

[30] Appendix 1- First interview with owner of North Al-Hail

[31] Appendix 6- Balance Sheet

2- Second interview with NAH owner discussed the plans needs to enter the hotel and hospital industry[32] which are:

- Estimated 10 new employees would need to be hired[33]
- Estimated 28 new machineries would need to be bought[34]
- Driving and Restraining forces for the force field analysis[35]

3- Questionnaire for NAH employees showed[36]:

- Widespread advantage for NAH to expand as 100% of all the employees are experienced with soft stich material clothing's and no employee is uncomfortable with the new stitching.

4- Interview with Hotel expert Karim William revealed[37]:

- Future of Tourism and hotels in Oman is positive, indication to go with expansion.
- The Kempinski Hotel procures their uniforms from Italy (externally) but are *"looking for more local companies as it will be more practical."*[38] This is a huge advantage for NAH as they can be their potential customers.
- Potential competitors 'white star tailors.'

5- Questionnaire for Hotel Industries showed[39]:

- 83.3% have seen positive growth in the tourism sector further implementing that NAH should expand into this industry.
- 83.3% would be interested in a new hotel uniform manufacture in Oman, this is a huge potential for NAH as they can gain customers.

---

[32] Appendix 2- Second interview with NAH owner about the financial and non-financial analysis
[33] Appendix 2- Second interview with NAH owner about the financial and non-financial analysis
[34] Appendix 2- Second interview with NAH owner about the financial and non-financial analysis
[35] Appendix 2- Second interview with NAH owner about the financial and non-financial analysis
[36] Appendix 4- Questionnaire for North Al-Hail employees
[37] Appendix 3 - Interview with a manager from the marketing department of hotels Mr. Karim William
[38] Appendix 3 - Interview with a manager from the marketing department of hotels Mr. Karim William
[39] Appendix 5- Questionnaire for Hotel Industries.

4: Analysis and Discussion:

4.1: Financial Analysis:

4.1.1: Ratio Analysis (NAH$)

A ratio analysis is a financial analysis tool used in the interpretation and assessment of NAH's financial statement to see whether it is strong enough to support the expansion of hotel and hospital industries.

A: Gross Profit Margin:

$$\frac{\text{Gross profit}}{\text{Total Revenue}} \times 100$$

$$\frac{44{,}128}{209{,}094} \times 100 = 21.10\%$$

B: Return on Capital Employed:

$$\frac{\text{Net Profit Before Interest \& Tax}}{\text{Capital Employed}} \times 100$$

$$\frac{2{,}466}{304{,}194} \times 100 = 0.81\%$$

C: Gearing Ratio:

$$\frac{\text{Loan Capital}}{\text{Capital Employed}} \times 100$$

$$\frac{0}{304{,}194} \times 100 = 0\%$$

D: Net Profit Margin:

$$\frac{\text{Net profit}}{\text{Total Revenue}} \times 100$$

$$\frac{2{,}434}{209{,}094} \times 100 = 1.16\%$$

The gross profit margin indicates the efficiency of a business to turn its raw materials into profits or income. The GPM helps decide the selling price of the product and services, standing at 21.10% it is considered a positive number. Expanding into this industry could potentially further increase NAH's GPM as compared to the average GPM of soft uniform retailers is the UK its around 50%[40], indicating the profitability of this industry. Although, the limitation of this is that the data is based on data in the UK, which may be different than Oman's data, due to the lack of resources on Oman.

[40] https://www.statista.com/statistics/673929/apparel-retailers-estimated-profit-margins-united-kingdom-uk/

The return of capital employed is the ratio which shows how much the capital of a business earns from a business, with 0.81% it is not an impressive figure as it doesn't reach 1% of the capital employed, thus, the management must re-plan their strategic business plan. However, with the gearing ratio standing at 0, it shows that NAH do not have any debts that needs to be funded. So, with a lot of unutilized funds, based on the gearing ratio NAH is in good shape to expand its company.

Because of the high competition in the uniform manufacturer industries, it led to lower Net profit margins and lower prices. NAH's current NPM stands at 1.16% which is relatively low in order to increase its NPM it must have a USP that differentiates itself from other competitors USP's.

4.1.2: Investment Appraisal:

Investment Appraisal refers to a range of quantitative decision-making techniques to assess investment projects[41]. This will help conclude whether NAH should invest in machinery and new employees in order to expanding to hotel and hospital industries.

The investment appraisal compromises of:

1- Payback Period

1- Payback Period:

The payback period is "a method of investment appraisal that estimates the time taken to recover the initial cash outlay on an investment."[42] The shorter the time taken to recover the initial cash outlay on an investment, the less risk of the investment. The payback period is important to conclude whether the investment should take place.

Payback Period = Cost of Investment / Annual Cash Flow

The forecast cashflow in Appendix 9[43], shows that NAH is able to pay back its investment costs of the machinery and the new employees in 10.9 months. This is acceptable and has a small risk as the initial project cost is approximately 27,195 OMR[44]. The new investment of machinery and employees will benefit NAH in the long run as more hotels and hospitals are predicted to open in Oman in the near future.

However, as stated by Adnan Al-Qadri, the sales revenue can be inconsistent because it depends on the number of uniforms ordered to manufacture and the materials of fabric used will differ in price[45]. Therefore, the forecasted cash may vary and the business should use different criteria's to accept the investment. With this investment, NAH should go ahead with this investment as 10.9 months is really acceptable.

[41] https://app.kognity.com/study/app/business-management-sl-hl/sid-73-cid-105972/book/the-big-pitc-id-8449
[42] https://app.kognity.com/study/app/business-management-sl-hl/sid-73-cid-105972/book/payback-period-id-8450
[43] Appendix 9- Investment Appraisal
[44] Appendix 9- Investment Appraisal
[45] Appendix 2- Second interview with NAH owner about the financial and non-financial analysis

4.2: Non- Financial Analysis:

4.2.1: Lewin's Force field Analysis

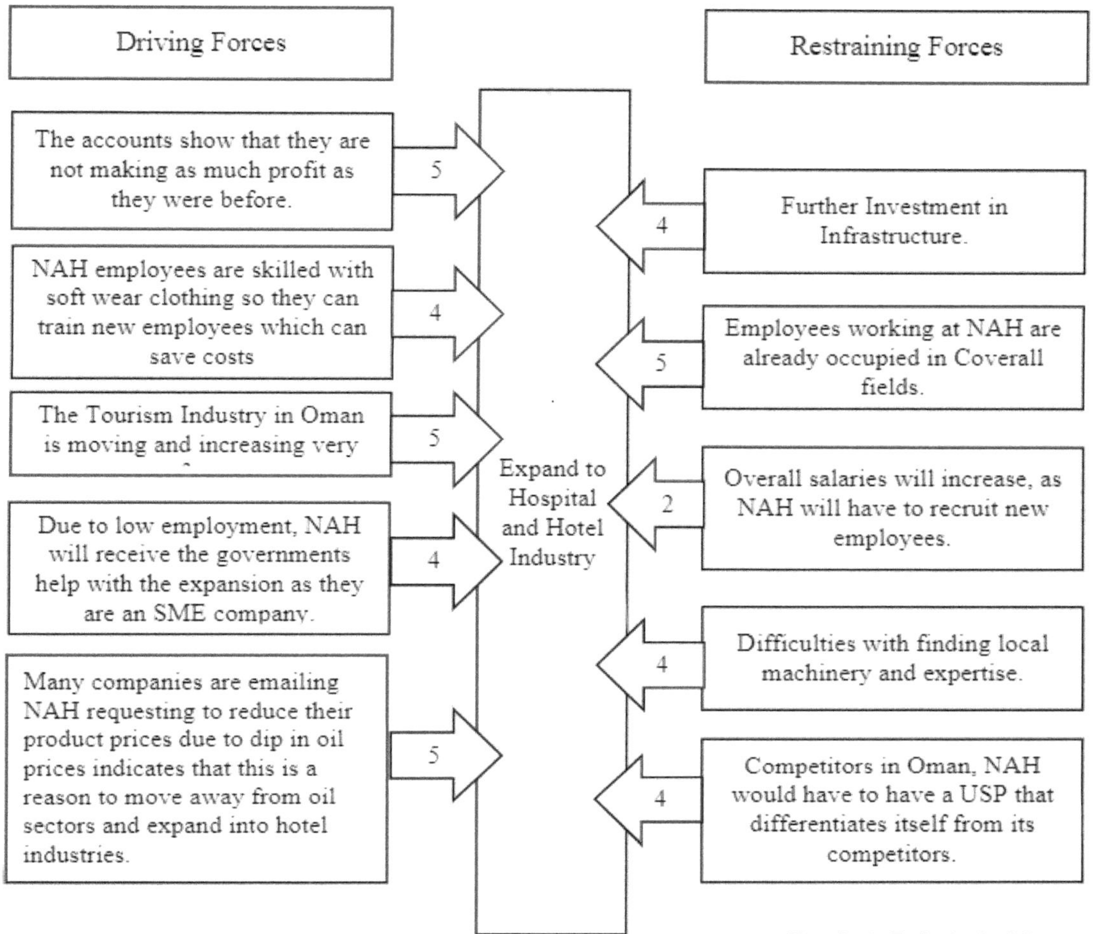

Total: 5+4+5+4+5= 23

Total: 4+5+2+4+4= 19

The director stated in the interview that his main reason for the consideration of expanding his business to hotel and hospital industries is to increase his profits as they had to reduce their prices for industrial coveralls due to the economic downturns[46]. Thus, improving profitability; it will also improve the firm's title as many new customers will associated with NAH especially now that the Tourism industry is expanding most hotels will prefer to supply from a local business hence why it is ranked 5/5.

[46] Appendix 8- Email send to North Al-Hail requesting reduction of prices.

NAH also has experience employees in both soft and hard wear industries, who can be used to train the new employees using on-the-job methods. This will reduce time and cost which can be allocated for recruitments and overall reduce labor costs.

Although, spending money on fixed assets (Machinery and increased salaries), generates income, it is considered as an opportunity cost as it is a huge investment which could potentially increase profits.

Driving forces outweighed the restraining forces, indicating that NAH should expand to hospital and hotel industries[47].

Conclusion:

In conclusion, all the tools and research have directed me towards a decision, NAH should expand its business to hotel industries first, then based on the success of the hotel industry expansion decide on whether to expand to hospital industries as well. I believe this will lead to NAH profits to increase.

The financial analysis based on the payback period 10.9 months[48] suggest low risk of investment. Moreover, the ratio analysis (GPM, GR) is all encouraging as the business is in good shape to expand.

The hotel industry survey[49] report suggests that although hotels do have a company where they supply their uniforms from, most of it is not local and they are interested in a local uniform manufacture which is a high potential for NAH to receive customers.

From the force field analysis, driving forces outweighs the restraining forces, the business can easily find solutions for the possible problem the expansion will cause for the business. Although, there are potential problems NAH may face from the expansion, it will cause their profits to increase significantly.

Recommendations:

- Extensive market research to understand the needs and wants of the potential customers in the uniform industry.
- Go ahead with expanding the business to hotel industries, however, with hospital industries it is concerning specially during the time of the pandemic and lake of resources available. Recommend to first focus on hotel industries as it is expanding quickly in Oman. Then later, based on how well NAH has succeed with the expansion of hotels, expand to hospital industry.
- NAH should could up with a USP that differentiates itself from other competitors USP.

[47] Appendix 2- Second interview with NAH owner about the financial and non-financial analysis
[48] Appendix 9- Investment Appraisal
[49] Appendix 5- Questionnaire for hotel industries

BIBLIOGRAPHY + APPENDICES OMITTED

7. EXAMPLE SEVEN (23/25)

Name: 'To What Extent Has Tesla's Implementation of a Manufacturing Plant In Shanghai Been Profitable?

Author: Anonymous

Session: May 2022

Level: SL

Table of contents

INTRODUCTION

Tesla Motors is an American manufacturer of luxurious electric vehicles founded in 2003 by a group of engineers.[1] The company does not only sell electric vehicles but also clean energy generation and storage products.[2] Tesla appeals to customers through its environmentally-friendly mission "to accelerate the world's transition to sustainable energy"[3] combining it with innovation and advanced technology which was achieved thanks to the considerable amount of money invested in research and development.

Tesla produces its vehicles at its factory in Fremont, California and the Gigafactory in Shanghai.[4] The Shanghai factory is the first outside of the US and begun production in December 2019. It has an annual production capacity of more than 450,000 Model 3 / Model Y vehicles[5] and it was mainly built to gain a foothold in China, the world's largest market for electric vehicles. But now, the factory has exceeded CEO Elon musk's expectations and is now the main exportation hub.[6] Only two years after the construction of the factory, the company reported a record net profit of $1.14 billion which is nearly ten times the $104 million in 2020 and a record of 201,250 cars delivered thanks to the strong demand from China[7]. Therefore, I decided to investigate:

To what extent has Tesla's implementation of a manufacturing plant in China been profitable?

---

[1] "About Tesla." *Tesla*, www.tesla.com/about.

[2] IBID

[3] IBID

[4] IBID

[5] Tesla. "Q2 2021 UPDATE ." *Tesla Investor Relations* , 26 July 2021, tesla-cdn.thron.com/static/ZBOUYO_TSLA_Q2_2021_Update_DJCVNJ.pdf?xseo=&response-content-disposition=inline%3Bfilename%3D%22q2_2021.pdf%22.

[6] IBID

[7] Yu, Yifan. "Tesla Makes Record Profit despite CHINA Headwind and Chip Crunch." *Nikkei Asia*, Nikkei Asia, 27 July 2021, asia.nikkei.com/Business/Technology/Tesla-makes-record-profit-despite-China-headwind-and-chip-crunch.

METHODOLOGY

This commentary will evaluate to what extent Tesla's decision to implement a manufacturing plant in Shanghai have been profitable. It is based on Tesla's Q1 2020 and the Q2 2021 quarterly reports, an article by Roberto Ferris analyzing Tesla's loss in shares after missing deliveries in 2019 and an analysis of Tesla's record profit in China by Yu Yifan. The following business tools will be used to analyze those documents and answer the question: A PESTLE analysis, Profitability ratios, Liquidity ratios and Return on capital employed (ROCE).

PESTLE ANALYSIS[8]

A PESTLE analysis is a framework used to evaluate a firm's external environment.[9]

Table 1: PESTLE analysis of Tesla in China

Political	**Economic**
• Initiatives taken by national and state governments to encourage manufacturing and sale of electric vehicles • These initiatives result in a reduction of taxes or a reduction in supply chains therefore leading to a higher gross profit.	• Improvement in global economy coupled with rise in sales of electric vehicles • Dip in prices of electric batteries to make electric vehicles affordable • The rise in sales of electric vehicles result in higher sales revenue for Tesla and with the dip in prices of electric vehicles, the cost of production will decrease allowing the company to reduce their prices
Social	**Technological**
• Improving preference of low carbon footprints and use of renewable energy	• Growing use of embedded technologies in automobiles • Advancement of technologies to reduce carbon footprint

[8] "Tesla Swot & PESTLE ANALYSIS: SWOT & PESTLE." *SWOT & PESTLE.com*, 4 Sept. 2020, https://www.swotandpestle.com/tesla-inc/#

[9] "Kognity." *App*, https://app.kognity.com/study/app/business-management-sl-2016/business-organisation-and-environment/external-environment /steeple-sociocultural-and-technological/

• Their customer base is widened leading to higher sales revenue	
Legal • Increased regulations related to automobile standards	**Environmental** • Increasing concern towards greenhouse gas emissions due to automobiles

This PESTLE analysis illustrates that Tesla's penetration of the Chinese market allowed them to reduce their cost of production and taxes due to initiatives taken by the government to encourage the sale of electric vehicles. The prices of electric batteries will also decrease lowering the cost of production and allowing higher gross profit to be achieved. The rise in sales of electric vehicles and the improving preference of the Chinese population for the use of renewable energy allowed the company to achieve higher sale revenues and widen its customer base.

All of these aspects of the Chinese market illustrate that Tesla is in the right market conditions to achieve profitability.

RATIO ANALYSIS

Liquidity Ratios

The current ratio and the acid test or quick ratio are indicators of the firm's ability to settle its short-term liabilities without the need to sell off any long-term assets.[10] The formulas are:[11]

$$Current\ ratio = \frac{current\ assets}{current\ liabilities}$$

$$Acid\ test\ ratio = \frac{Current\ assets - Stock}{Current\ liabilities}$$

Table 2: Tesla's end of year liquidity data from 2019 to 2021[12, 13]

(In millions of USD $ except ratios)			
Year	2019	2020	2021
Quarter	Q4	Q4	Q2
Current assets	12,103	26,717	24,693
Current liabilities	10,667	14,248	16,371
Inventory	3,552	4,101	4,733
Current ratio	1,13	1,87	1,5
Acid-test ratio	0,8	1,58	1,21

Table 2 reveals that in 2019, Tesla did not have an ideal liquidity. The company had a current ratio of 1.13:1 which is below the general prudent accounting

10 "Kognity." *App*, https://app.kognity.com/study/app/business-management-sl-2016/finance-and-accounts/profitability-and-liquidity-ratio-analysis/liquidity-ratios/.
11 "Kognity." *App*, https://app.kognity.com/study/app/business-management-sl-2016/finance-and-accounts/profitability-and-liquidity-ratio-analysis/liquidity-ratios/.
12 Tesla. "Tesla Q1 2020 Update." *Tesla Investor Relations* , 29 Apr. 2020, tesla-cdn.thron.com/static/HZTKGL_TSLA_Update_Letter_2020-1Q_VGVL6F.pdf
13 Tesla. "Q2 2021 UPDATE ." *Tesla Investor Relations* , 26 July 2021, tesla-cdn.thron.com/static/ZBOUYO_TSLA_Q2_2021_Update_DJCVNJ.pdf?xseo=&response-content-disposition=inline%3Bfilename%3D%22q2_2021.pdf%22.

recommendation of 1.5 to 2.[14] It means that if the company pay off its short-term debts with its current assets, it won't have sufficient cash remained to continue its core business activities even if they sell the entirety of their stock.

However, in 2020, the company achieved an impressive ratio of 1.87:1. This increase is explained by the increase cash and cash equivalents. In 2020, their cash increased by nearly 309% YoY. In 2021, the ratios decreased slightly due to production and reputational challenges[15] which affected production capacity therefore cash. Also, the company made a repayment worth of $1.6B in debt and finance lease.[16] The company has many long-term debts that it has to repay.

The implementation of the Shanghai plant allowed Tesla to achieve higher ratios due to an impressive increase in cash and cash equivalents of more than 300% in one year ($6.2B to $19.3B)[17].

Efficiency ratios

The Return on Capital Employed (ROCE) is used to measure how efficiently a company generates profits from its capital employed.[18] It indicates the percentage of profit that each dollar of capital employed generates.[19]

It is calculated as follow:[20]

$$Return\ on\ Capital\ Employed = \frac{Net\ profit\ before\ interest\ and\ tax\ (EBIT)}{Capital\ employed} \times 100$$

$$Where\ capital\ employed = long - term\ liabilities + share\ capital + accumulated\ retained\ profit$$

[14] "Kognity." *App*, https://app.kognity.com/study/app/business-management-sl-2016/finance-and-accounts/profitability-and-liquidity-ratio-analysis/liquidity-ratios/.

[15] Yu, Yifan. "Tesla Makes Record Profit despite CHINA Headwind and Chip Crunch." *Nikkei Asia*, Nikkei Asia, 27 July 2021, asia.nikkei.com/Business/Technology/Tesla-makes-record-profit-despite-China-headwind-and-chip-crunch.

[16] Tesla. "Q2 2021 UPDATE ." *Tesla Investor Relations* , 26 July 2021, tesla-cdn.thron.com/static/ZBOUYO_TSLA_Q2_2021_Update_DJCVNJ.pdf?xseo=&response-content-disposition=inline%3Bfilename%3D%22q2_2021.pdf%22.

[17] IBID

[18] "Kognity." *App*, https://app.kognity.com/study/app/business-management-sl-2016/finance-and-accounts/profitability-and-liquidity-ratio-analysis/liquidity-ratios/.

[19] IBID

[20] IBID

Table 3: Tesla's ROCE quarterly from 2019 to 2021[21] [22]

(In millions of USD $ except percentages)

Year	2019				2020				2021	
Quarter	Q1	Q2	Q3	Q4	Q1	Q2	Q3	Q4	Q1	Q2
Net profit	-522	-167	261	359	283	327	809	575	594	1,312
Capital employed	19.67	22,283	22,649	23,642	25,264	25,805	32,589	37.9	38,095	38,775
ROCE	(2.65%)	(0.74%)	1.15%	1.51%	1.12%	1.26%	2.48%	1.51%	1.55%	3.38%

Table 3 indicates that Tesla has an increasing efficiency over time. In the beginning of 2019, the company had a negative ROCE meaning that each $100 dollars of capital employed will generate a loss. The company faced deliveries issues in the first quarter of 2019. They delivered 63,000 cars out of the 76,000 deliveries expected.[23] The company justified itself by saying that "it was challenging to deliver cars around the world when they were manufactured only in one factory meaning that production could continue to outpace deliveries"[24] which resulted in a negative net profit (Loss).

However, from mid-2019, with the implementation of the Shanghai plant, the company's ROCE started increasing. The higher ROCE was achieved in Q2 2021 due to higher production and deliveries resulting in a higher net profit.

The increasing ROCE due to an increase in net profit illustrates that the company's efficiency has been increasing since the implementation of the Shanghai plant.

---

[21] Tesla. "Tesla Q1 2020 Update." *Tesla Investor Relations* , 29 Apr. 2020, tesla-cdn.thron.com/static/HZTKGL_TSLA_Update_Letter_2020-1Q_VGVL6F.pdf

[22] Tesla. "Q2 2021 UPDATE ." *Tesla Investor Relations* , 26 July 2021, tesla-cdn.thron.com/static/ZBOUYO_TSLA_Q2_2021_Update_DJCVNJ.pdf?xseo=&response-content-disposition=inline%3Bfilename%3D%22q2_2021.pdf%22

[23] Roberto, Ferris. "Tesla Shares Fall by as Much as 10.7% after Deliveries Miss by a Wide Margin." *CNBC*, CNBC, 29 May 2019, www.cnbc.com/2019/04/04/tesla-q1-2019-production-and-delivery-numbers.html.

[24] IBID

Profitability Ratios

The Gross Profit Margin (GPM) and the Net Profit Margin (NPM) are profitability ratios that indicates how well a business is doing. It is used to show the difference in profitability of Tesla from 2019 to 2021. [25]

They are calculated by the formulas:[26]

$$Gross\ profit\ margin = \frac{Gross\ profit}{Sales\ revenue} \times 100$$

$$Net\ profit\ margin = \frac{Net\ profit\ before\ interest\ and\ tax\ (EBIT)}{Sales\ revenue} \times 100$$

Table 4: Tesla's profitability data quarterly from 2019 to 2021[27] [28]

(in millions of USD $ except percentages)

Year	2019				2020				2021	
Quarter	Q1	Q2	Q3	Q4	Q1	Q2	Q3	Q4	Q1	Q2
Sales revenues	4,541	6,35	6,303	7,384	5,985	6,036	8,771	10,744	10,389	11,958
Gross profit	566	921	1,191	1,391	1,234	1,267	2,063	1,066	2,215	2,884
Gross profit margin	12.5%	14.5%	18.9%	18.8%	20.6%	21.0%	23.5%	19.2%	21.3%	24.1%
Net profit	-522	-167	261	359	283	327	809	575	594	1,312
Net profit margin (Loss)	(11.5%)	(2.6%)	4.1%	4.9%	4.7%	5.4%	9.2%	5.4%	5.7%	11.0%

Table 4 shows that Tesla has been experiencing increasing revenue, GPM and NPM since the third quarter of 2019. In Q1 and Q2 2019, the company experienced a loss due to delivery issues. But, with the implementation of the Shanghai plant, production

---

[25] "Kognity." *App*, https://app.kognity.com/study/app/business-management-sl-2016/finance-and-accounts/profitability-and-liquidity-ratio-analysis/liquidity-ratios/.

[26] IBID

[27] Tesla. "Tesla Q1 2020 Update." *Tesla Investor Relations*, 29 Apr. 2020, tesla-cdn.thron.com/static/HZTKGL_TSLA_Update_Letter_2020-1Q_VGVL6F.pdf

[28] Tesla. "Q2 2021 UPDATE." *Tesla Investor Relations*, 26 July 2021, tesla-cdn.thron.com/static/ZBOUYO_TSLA_Q2_2021_Update_DJCVNJ.pdf?xseo=&response-content-disposition=inline%3Bfilename%3D%22q2_2021.pdf%22.

capacity and delivery rate increased significantly. Out of the 206,421 vehicles produced, 201,304 were delivered[29] which is a significant increase from the prior years. Gross profit went up by 128%[30] explained by the reduction of the cost of productions. The company uses local parts manufactured by Chinese suppliers, rather than importing them from the US and paying additional tariffs such as importation costs and taxes. Which lowers the cost of production. 30% of the parts used are local but they plan to increase it to a 100% which will surely double the gross profits and the sales revenue as the price will be lower. The increase in gross profit resulted in an increase in net profit as the operating expenses remained slightly the same.

CONCLUSION

Based on the PESTLE analysis, Tesla seems to be in the right market conditions due to supportive political policies regarding taxes and regulations as well availability of strong local manufacturers. The plant increased the production capacity and helped to solve the delivery issues that the company faced in 2019. Additionally, the company experienced a significant increase of: The Gross Profit Margin and the Net Profit Margin form 12,5% to 24,1% and (11,5%) to 11% respectively; the Return on Capital Employed from (2,65%) to 3,38%; and the Current ratio and Acid-test ration from 1,13 to 1,5 and 0,8 to 1,21. However, their sales dropped in Q1 2021 due to criticism regarding the cars and increasing competition in the automobile market. Overall, based on the PESTLE and ratios analysis, Tesla's implementation of the Shanghai plant has been profitable to a great extent.

---

[29] Tesla. "Q2 2021 UPDATE ." *Tesla Investor Relations* , 26 July 2021, tesla-cdn.thron.com/static/ZBOUYO_TSLA_Q2_2021_Update_DJCVNJ.pdf?xseo=&response-content-disposition=inline%3Bfilename%3D%22q2_2021.pdf%22.

[30] IBID

BIBLIOGRAPHY + APPENDICES OMITTED

www.ingramcontent.com/pod-product-compliance
Lightning Source LLC
Chambersburg PA
CBHW041512210926
51847CB00011B/122
* 9 7 8 1 9 9 9 6 1 1 5 8 3 *